GEORGE MASON AND THE LEGACY OF CONSTITUTIONAL LIBERTY

An Examination of the Influence of George Mason on the American Bill of Rights

GEORGE MASON AND THE LEGACY OF CONSTITUTIONAL LIBERTY

An Examination of The Influence of George Mason on the American Bill of Rights

by

Dr. Donald J. Senese
Editor

Introductory Comments
Ms. Elise Murray, *Chairman*
Fairfax County History Commission

Contributors

Dr. Edward W. Chester
Dr. Robert P. Davidow
Mr. Joseph Horrell
Justice Sandra Day O'Connor

Dr. Josephine F. Pacheco
Dr. Diane D. Pikcunas
Dr. Robert A. Rutland
Dr. Donald J. Senese

A publication of the Fairfax County History Commission in cooperation with the Fairfax County Commission on the Bicentennial of the United States Constitution, 1989.

© This publication is copyrighted by the Fairfax County History Commission. 1989

Library of Congress Catalog Card Number: 89-85565
ISBN 0-9623905-1-8

Additional copies of this publication may be purchased from The Map and Publications Center, Fairfax County, 4100 Chain Bridge Road, Fairfax, Virginia 22030, (703) 246-2974. Additional information can be obtained by calling (703) 237-4881.

TABLE OF CONTENTS

                                                                               Page

Introductory Commentary – *Elise Murray* 7
Introduction – *Donald J. Senese* 8
Attributions 12

I.   **The Early Years**
      "George Mason and the Preparation for Leadership"
          by *Diane D. Pikcunas* 15
      "George Mason and the Fairfax Court"
          by *Joseph Horrell* 32

II.   **The Constitution Years**
      "George Mason and the Constitution"
          by *Josephine F. Pacheco* 61
      "George Mason's 'Objections' and the Bill of Rights"
          by *Robert A. Rutland* 75
      "George Mason on the Tension Between Majority Rule
      and Minority Rights"
          by *Robert P. Davidow* 82

III.   **The Lasting Influence**
      "George Mason – His Lasting Influence"
          by *Sandra Day O'Connor* 117
      "George Mason – Influence Beyond the United States"
          by *Edward W. Chester* 128
      "George Mason – Why the Forgotten Founding Father"
          by *Donald J. Senese* 147

IV.   **Appendices – Documents Protecting Individual Rights**
      "Final Draft of the Virginia Declaration of Rights" 155
      "Objections to this Constitution of Government"
          by *George Mason* 158
      United States: "Bill of Rights, U.S. Constitution" 161
      France: "Declaration of the Rights of Man and
          the Citizen" 163
      United Nations: "Universal Declaration of
          Human Rights" 166

Biographical Sketches of Contributors 181

Index 185

Fairfax County History Commission

Elise R. Murray, *Chairman*
Donald J. Senese, *Vice-Chairman*
Abbie Edwards, *Treasurer*

Rev. Clinton W. Austin • Beatrice M. Prescott
Clark B. Hall • Patrick Reed • Jack L. Hiller
Milburn Sanders • William A. Klene • Edith M. Sprouse
Virginia B. Peters • Charles L. Shoup • Mayo S. Stuntz

Members Emeritus

C.J.S. Durham   Donie Rieger

Advisors

Bernard N. Boston   Warren E. Barry
Denzil O. Evans   Nan Netherton

Fairfax County Board of Supervisors

Audrey Moore, *Chairman*
Martha V. Pennino, *Vice Chairman*

Joseph Alexander • Sharon Bulova • Thomas M. Davis III
Katherine K. Hanley • Gerald W. Hyland • Elaine McConnell • Lilla Richards

J. Hamilton Lambert, *County Executive*

Fairfax County Commission on the Bicentennial of the United States Constitution

Mary Lee Link Allen, *Chairman*
C.J.S. Durham, *Chairman Emeritus*
Pat Brady, *Vice-Chairman*
John Riley, *Vice-Chairman*
Paul Terpak, *Treasurer*
D'Anne Evans, *Corresponding Secretary*

Gerald W. Hyland • William A. Harper • Patricia E. Archer
Richard Korink • Robert W. Beers • John P. Liberty • Orville T. Bonner
S. Branson Marley • Stella Bryans-Munson • James McConville
Glenn C. Bowman • Josephine F. Pacheco • Elizabeth David
Clyde E. Phelps • Thomas M. Durbin • Donald J. Senese
Anthony P. Dzierski • Audrey E. S. Williams • Mariella H. Gosnell

Introductory Comments

The Fairfax County History Commission is pleased to present this special collection of essays on one of our most important Founding Fathers: *George Mason and the Legacy of Constitutional Liberty: An Examination of the Influence of George Mason on the American Bill of Rights*. We hope that these essays will inspire a greater knowledge of George Mason and the United States Constitution as well as a greater appreciation of Fairfax County's role in the establishment of the new nation, the United States of America. This contribution has lasted over two hundred years and has been a great influence on other nations as well. We especially appreciate the work of one of our commission members, Dr. Donald J. Senese, who edited this work and the staff of Gunston Hall and members of the Fairfax County Commission on the Bicentennial of the United States Constitution who assisted in its final preparation.

The members of the Fairfax County History Commission hope that we can stimulate in our school children and our adults a greater awareness of our history and the importance of knowing it as a guide to our future. We believe this work will go a long way toward that goal.

Elise Murray, *Chairman*
Fairfax County History Commission

Editor's Introduction

I am pleased to have the opportunity to edit a series of outstanding articles and essays on one of our least known but most important Founding Fathers, George Mason of Gunston Hall, Fairfax County, Virginia.

The celebration of the Bicentennial of the United States Constitution extends from September 17, 1987 to the ratification of the Bill of Rights, December 15, 1991.

It is appropriate that we examine this crucial period through the career of George Mason, whose leadership contributed to the American Revolution and to the Constitutional Convention. After Mason helped to create the Constitution, he refused to sign it and proceeded to lead efforts against its ratification in Virginia. First on his list of objections was that there was no declaration of rights. The final event we celebrate during the Bicentennial — the Ratification of the Bill of Rights, the first ten amendments to the U.S. Constitution — owed much to George Mason who wrote the Virginia Declaration of Rights, whose ideas influenced Thomas Jefferson's Declaration of Independence, who fought for a Bill of Rights in the Constitutional Convention, and who actively supported its addition later when James Madison, an opponent of the Bill of Rights in the Constitutional Convention, introduced such a measure in the First Congress and guided it to final passage. History is full of such ironies.

One can go down in flames yet rise from the ashes. Burdened by ill health and responsibilities of family and farms, George Mason died on October 7, 1792 at the age of 67. However, he lived long enough to see his dream realized. He died less than a year after the Bill of Rights was added to the U.S. Constitution. We hope that the reader will find an adventure in learning as he or she reads *George Mason and the Legacy of Constitutional Liberty: An Examination of the*

Influence of George Mason on the American Bill of Rights.

The authors accept George Mason as an influential figure in American and even world history. He is especially appreciated in recent years as we become more conscious of the importance of civil rights and civil liberties and the need for these guarantees, in our country and in other nations. However, not all the contributors agree on the interpretations of his role, activities, and significance. This diversity enables the reader to make his or her individual judgments. The authors represent a diversity of fields and professions — from businessman/historian to an elementary school principal, college professors and even a law professor, to an associate justice of the U.S. Supreme Court. Their biographical sketches reveal the wealth of talent we have contributing to this project.

I have attempted to organize the book into three broad categories based upon Mason's career: the early years; the Constitution years; and the lasting influence. A fourth section contains key documents of individual rights, all bearing the influence of George Mason.

The examination of Mason in these three phases helps us put his career in perspective. Diane D. Pikcunas examines the setting of his career, the influences on Mason, and the beginnings of his involvement in politics which bring his career to his emergence into national prominence during the break with England. Joseph Horrell gives us a description of his talents and examines his role in the Fairfax court. Both essays show the development of Mason's knowledge of government and politics as a preparation for his role in the coming struggle over political rights of the American colonists.

The section on the Constitution years examines the critical role Mason played in the creation of the document we consider our fundamental law. Josephine F. Pacheco focuses on Mason's role in the Constitutional Convention while Robert A. Rutland considers his objections to the Constitution and the question of a bill of rights. Robert P. Davidow abstracts a broader question inherent in Mason's philosophy: the tension between majority rule and minority rights.

The final section places Mason's influence in the broader perspective of a political philosopher whose influence carries down to our day and will continue in future years. Supreme Court Justice Sandra Day O'Connor shows that Mason's ideas are cited throughout our history in arguments and cases heard before our highest tribunal, the United States Supreme Court. Edward W. Chester follows Mason's ideas beyond the time he lived to discover his influence on such documents as France's Declaration of the Rights of Man and the Citizen, the constitutions of new and old nations during the nineteenth and twentieth centuries and the United Nations Universal Declaration of Human Rights. Finally, I examine the ebb and flow of history which have left Mason an almost forgotten Founding Father. Perhaps this work will help to reverse that historical injustice.

Thanks are due many for this work and I want to mention the most noteworthy. Thanks goes to the Fairfax County Board of Supervisors for their generous funding of the history commissions, the Fairfax County History Commission and the Fairfax County Commission on the Bicentennial of the U.S. Constitution, which made this work possible. I appreciate the support of Elise Murray, Chairman of the Fairfax History Commission, who is always a tower of strength for any Fairfax County History Commission project; the support and assistance of Mary Lee Allen who, in her dual role as Chairman of the Fairfax County Commission on the Bicentennial of the United States Constitution and Assistant Director of Gunston Hall, has provided important support and guidance; and Josephine F. Pacheco of George Mason University and the Fairfax County Bicentennial Commission who supplied the original suggestion for the format of this work, thus easing the work of the editor. Thanks to the Board of Regents of Gunston Hall for allowing the reprint of the article by Dr. Davidow on which the Board holds the copyright. I appreciate the cooperation of the authors who contributed and the publications which granted permission to reprint their articles in order to bring them to the attention of a wider audience. Special recognition goes to the contributors of two original chapters in this work, Diane D. Pikcunas and Edward W. Chester, who put aside other work to assist in this endeavor. Suzanne S. Levy aided us by providing the resources on George Mason from the Virginia Room of the Fairfax City Library, Fairfax County. Nanette Gibbs of the Sherwood Branch of the Fairfax County Library helped me in a search for documents which adds to the significance of this work.

The views expressed in these articles are those of the authors and do not reflect the views or opinions of the sponsoring organizations.

Donald J. Senese
Vice-Chairman Fairfax County History Commission and Chairman, George Mason Publication Project

Attributions

"George Mason and the Fairfax Court," by Joseph Horrell, is reprinted with permission of the author and *The Virginia Magazine of History and Biography* (October, 1983), Volume 91, No. 4., pp. 418-439.

"George Mason and the Constitution," by Josephine F. Pacheco, is reprinted with permission from the author and from the *New York State Bar Journal* (October, 1987), pp. 10-17.

"George Mason's 'Objections' and the Bill of Rights," by Robert A. Rutland is reprinted with the permission of the author and *this Constitution: A Bicentennial Chronicle*, published by Project '87 of the American Historical Association and the American Political Science Association, (Spring/Summer, 1988), pp. 11-13

"George Mason — His Lasting Influence," by Sandra Day O'Connor, Remarks at Gunston Hall, October 3, 1987 is reprinted with permission from the author Associate Justice Sandra Day O'Connor, U.S. Supreme Court.

"George Mason on the Tension Between Majority Rule and Minority Rights," by Robert P. Davidow, is reprinted with permission of the Board of Regents of Gunston Hall who hold the copyright, the author Dr. Robert P. Davidow, and the *George Mason University Law Review*, Volume 10 (1987), pp. 1-26.

The articles by Diane D. Pikcunas, Edward W. Chester, and Donald J. Senese are original articles prepared for this publication.

GEORGE MASON AND THE LEGACY OF CONSTITUTIONAL LIBERTY

An Examination of the Influence of George Mason on the American Bill of Rights

Section 1: The Early Years

"George Mason and the Preparation for Leadership"
by
Diane D. Pikcunas

"George Mason and the Fairfax Court"
by
Joseph Horrell

GEORGE MASON: THE PREPARATION FOR LEADERSHIP

by Diane D. Pikcunas

Few but scholars might realize that the Bill of Rights was not part of the original Constitution or fully appreciate the role played by a planter-statesman in America's Golden Age, who made the declaration of rights as his personal crusade, George Mason.

The Bicentennial celebration of the United States Constitution from its adoption on September 17, 1787 to the ratification of the first ten amendments known as the Bill of Rights in December of 1791, serves as a tribute to the great statesmen who helped write, debate, adopt, and guide this basic charter of our government to completion. The names of the major actors are known to us — George Washington, John Adams, James Madison, James Monroe, and Benjamin Franklin among others. Some of these retained a prominent place in public memory because of other earlier achievements (e.g., Benjamin Franklin for his role as scientist and publisher) or future achievements (e.g., election to the presidency, like Washington and Adams, Madison, and Monroe). Other individuals played important roles in the evolution of the Constitution and the establishment of the governmental system which has endured in our country for over two hundred years; but because their main role was conducted in the shadow of these few, great men are today almost unknown to our modern generation. One such individual was George Mason of Gunston Hall, Fairfax County, Virginia.

Mason's contribution to constitutional development will be the focus of other essays, discussing his political thought and career, his contributions to the debate in the Constitutional Convention, his objections to the final document, his refusal to sign it and his lobbying against its ratification, his influence in having the Bill of Rights added, and finally, the enduring legacy of his political thought, both in the United States and abroad, over these past two centuries. The focus of this essay will be on the early influences in his life, the development of his career, and how he made his debut on the national stage. This early background reveals how he had achieved a position of respect and influence by the time of the American Revolution, the writing of the Virginia Constitution, and the movement toward writing the U.S. Constitution.

George Mason was first of all a devoted family man who was widowed and left with nine children (although he did later remarry); but he was also the possessor of a large plantation which he nurtured with care and which he devoted much attention concerning its many details of management. The experience of running and governing a large estate helped to prepare Mason, as well as other plantation owners of the time, for the responsibilities of local, state, and national government. Mason had priorities but the desire to travel and to undertake extensive governmental responsibilities in distant Williamsburg or Richmond or Philadelphia was not one of them. He did not shirk from governmental responsibility but he preferred that others representing his views would undertake these time-consuming and arduous tasks.

Mason enjoyed debating ideas and was well-acquainted with the leading political theories of the past and those of his age. When called upon to exercise governmental responsibilities, he performed well. At times he may have been too blunt, too direct, too forceful in enunciating his views to be a successful politician. However, his devotion to home and property was paramount — a feature of his life which led one biographer to label him 'a reluctant statesman.'[1]

An examination of Mason's early life reveals him as very much a product of his age — a large landowner who managed his plantation successfully, interacting congenially with his neighbors and colleagues such as George Washington at nearby Mount Vernon. However, Mason assumed a leading role in the revolutionary and constitutional debates of his age.

The reconstruction of George Mason's character, life, and views should begin with an examination of his surroundings — the colony of Virginia.

The Virginia colony had been founded during the great age of exploration, discovery, and speculation. It was an age of adventure and liberation, as a new philosophy of government and international finance encouraged governments to undertake missions of colonization to new lands; establish colonies through settlement of its own citizens abroad; and establish these colonies as economically viable units sufficient to guarantee their own economic prosperity while benefitting the mother country through its extension of power and trade. Great rivalries took place among the leading powers of Europe seeking wealth, power, and dominion. Nations such as England, France, Spain, and Portugal extended their rivalries across the seas with a focus on domination of the American continent.

A different approach was apparent among the founding of the colonies. The Spanish Empire had a centralized origin with its colonies completely financed by the Spanish Crown, a system which gave the Spanish government full responsibility and control and underwrote any financial uncertainty. England took a different approach which was more speculative and less secure financially. Jamestown in Virginia was founded in 1607 and became the first permanent settlement.

Virginia had been founded not as a Crown-financed colony but as a stock-holding company, which made it a dubious and speculative financial venture with uncertain backing. If finances ran short, the colonial venture could collapse. The British settlers in Jamestown had to endure food shortages, threats from Indian attacks, and the ever present spectre of illness and diseases but managed to survive. Their difficulties likely contributed to a sterner and more determined character among the English settlers.

Aside from its adventuresome origins, Virginia, differed

from the Spanish colonies in another way — its source of income. Spain built colonies which could become trading centers, sending goods back to the mother country. Virginia became a replica of the mother country — a settlement for farmers seeking a permanent home in the New World. Fortunately, Virginia discovered a crop which became the source of its economic validity. One could say in a true sense that the Virginia colony was built on smoke — that successful crop was tobacco.[2]

If we are to understand George Mason, we need to comprehend the growth of the landowner class in Virginia which became both the economic and political power in Virginia. The colony had its craftsman and its manufactures group but its land owning class dominated its society and the commonwealth retained its rural and landed origins. The power which a landowner such as Mason exercised over the political and economic sphere became clear as the society developed. Historian Louis Rubin describes the developing society which allowed the landowners to assume a governing role in society:

> There was comparatively little detailed supervision by the royal governor and his administration, and such towns as began developing were little more than places where the court could meet. The county governments quickly assumed a powerful role in Virginia life; local autonomy became a fixed feature of the society, with the elected burgesses chosen geographically to represent the wishes and speak to the needs of a citizenry living and working away from the seat of the King's government.[3]

As Virginia grew its landed aristocracy continued to serve as its leaders. The establishment of slavery in Virginia ensured the prosperity of its landed class and their dominance. Slaves came to Virginia in 1619. This slave-owning aristocracy wielded prime influence in the House of Burgesses by the early 18th century. Scions of great families came from England to Virginia, bringing their status with them; a middle class or bourgeois aristocracy also became a component of Virginia society. The establishment of prominent families who dominated Virginia's politics for decades became apparent during this time — the Lees, the Byrds, and the Randolphs. These individuals of both status and power were energetic in the pursuit of wealth but also possessed a sense of duty and responsibility in their own governance and the governance of others.

A limited aristocracy would not remain long. During the 1730s, the 1740s, and the 1750s, the planter society in Virginia enlarged its base moving toward a more republican form of government. Though the larger planters still held influence, a generation change had occurred as the sons of these large planters found themselves living in a more diverse society, consisting of large tobacco planters and small farmers. The Virginia political scene underwent a change as power shifted from an appointive Council to an elected body, the House of Burgesses.

Those interested in obtaining seats in the House of Burgesses, the representative assembly, had to campaign and win support from two important groups — the large landowners and the small landowners. These democratic tendencies moderated the Virginia aristocracy and enabled a new group of leaders to be trained for the later break with England.[4]

Other studies have confirmed the emergence of these democratic tendencies in Virginia society, and thus the discovery that some aspects considered aristocratic were actually democratic. A more democratic form of government was evolving and in Virginia the franchise, representative government and elements of democracy emerged through the proceedings of the Council as well as through the limits on the role of the governor. In the later opposition to Britain, the situation did not pose a distinct democratic group against an aristocratic opposition. The situation resembled more one of liberals and conservatives who had different views of man and of the nature of society, who joined together against

Britain in common opposition and who were content to debate their differences after the struggle with Britain was won.[5]

This Virginia society was the birthplace of George Mason. An examination of the Mason family gives us a view of Virginia society and the setting in which his political views evolved.

Place and location were important, and some attention should be given to the specific geographic location of the Mason family property. The Mason family lived on a peninsula which was originally known as Doeg Neck and then later became Mason's Neck. This area was surrounded on three sides by water. The Masons, along with other families like the Cockburns and the Masseys, lived on the Neck in a community somewhat apart from Fairfax County.

The first George Mason (1660-1716), the grandfather of the subject of our study, was himself the son of a George Mason who been a Royalist immigrant, who settled in present day Stafford County about thirty miles below Dogue or Doeg Neck. It was George Mason's grandfather who moved to the Dogue Neck region, an area of high risk, subject to Indian attacks (e.g., the Doeg and Necostin Indians resided in this region). Rangers or individuals committed to protection were needed to patrol and provide safety. George Mason settled this area and received an appointment as a county lieutenant, a commander in chief of the rangers (about 11 men with horses and firearms). This ancestor of George Mason died in 1716.

George Mason's father (1690-1735), bearing the same name, also became a county lieutenant and helped provide protection for the area. As was the case with some permanent landowners, he was elected a member of the representative body, the House of Burgesses in 1718. He had inherited the land in Virginia and moved to acquire additional land. He married, and his son, George Mason, who was to take such a prominent role in the debates of the American Revolution and the U.S. Constitution, was born in 1725. However, tragedy struck in 1735 — while crossing the Potomac his boat was upset and he drowned.

Young George Mason was only 10 years old at the time of his father's death. As his father left no will, George Mason became heir at this early age to all his father's property — including the Dogue Neck Plantation, which contained about 4,000 acres, the Occoquan Plantation (which was later called Woodbridge), and the Chickamuxon Plantation in Charles County, Maryland. (A public ferry linked Occoquan Plantation to Dogue Neck).[6]

Interest in George Mason's career has lagged over the years because of the lack of knowledge on his early years in comparison with the knowledge we possess of the other Founding Fathers. We can agree on the basic facts. Mason at the age of 25 married Ann Eilbeck of Charles County, Maryland in 1750; five years later he began to build the famous Gunston Hall, named for the home of his maternal ancestors, the Fowkes of Staffordshire in England. William Buckland did the interior of the house and this interior featured delicate and even elaborate decoration. By 1758, Gunston Hall was completed like similar plantations of the day with a school house on its premises, stables for horses and poultry houses, cattle pens and a hay yard, living quarters for the servants, pasture for livestock, orchards with fruit trees, and a road leading down to the landing where items arriving by boat could be received.[7]

Mason served as master over the plantation which bore the resemblance to an autonomous governing unit. The plantation was organized so that its resources could be used most efficiently. The slaves were trained in skills, such as coopers, blacksmiths, tanners, shoemakers, and weavers. A cycle of production was available as the woods supplied timber and plank for the carpenters, the cattle supplied skin for the tanners and curriers (and even the shoemakers), the fields supplied cotton and flax for the weavers and spinners, and charcoal was available from the woods for the blacksmiths. Clothes as well as shoes were made on the plantation. The animals which were slaughtered were preserved by the salting process and packed away for later use.[8]

George Mason took great pride in managing his plantation. He did not employ regular clerks but kept the books himself, and supervised the estate with the help of possibly one or two slaves. Mason's devotion to his plantation limited the time he had available for leisure and for reading. While little is known of his early education, Mason was not a lawyer but was well read, interested in books and political ideas. He had access to one of the better supplied libraries, that of John Mercer, who had married his aunt.[9]

This leader in Virginia had a comfortable but very fulfilling life. By the age of 50, Mason had a successful plantation, a helpful wife, and a family of 9 children. In March of 1773, a major tragedy occurred similar to the sudden death of his father — his beloved wife of 23 years Ann died following a long illness. Now Mason had the responsibility not only for the plantation but of nine children; he had to fit reading and other business enterprises into his spare time.[10]

One aspect of Mason's character and personality deserves attention. He had a disposition not well suited for a political figure. Accounts of the time indicate that he was forthright in his views, even blunt, and the gout with which he was afflicted seems likely to have added to his natural irritability. He bore burdens readily but since it appears from his letters that he rarely delegated responsibility, he only added to his own already heavy load. Besides his business dealings (including tenure as treasurer of a complex business arrangement with the Ohio Company), Mason had much to occupy himself with in his concern for family, home, and health.[11]

The significant role Mason would fill will be covered by others but his early emergence into politics deserves attention. In 1748, while still in his early twenties, he unsuccessfully sought a seat in the House of Burgesses from Fairfax County. A decade later he was successful in his quest, serving there from 1758-1761.[12]

Mason seemed at this time to acquire a lifelong aversion to active service in government office. He disliked the exchange of political favors, known as logrolling, and the seemingly endless oratory he found in the House of Burgesses. He thus decided that this type of service should be left to others, while he would be satisfied to influence events by contact with and advice to friends. He decided on a short career in the House of Burgesses, and looked forward to returning to full-time management of his estate.[13]

The other roles Mason filled in the coming political battle for independence deserve mention. Although he may not have held an official title, his wisdom, his advice, and his active participation were sought by those who did. He participated in the efforts to resist enforcement of the Stamp Act, the British measure which levied a tax on certain commercial documents, and he engaged in this effort during the years 1765-1766. By 1769 he was active in shaping the nonimportation agreements which resisted the new taxes imposed on the colonies by the British Parliament. He wrote, in 1773, the "Extracts of Virginia Charters" which upheld land claims. In 1774, as Virginians began organizing opposition to Britain, he contributed to the writing of the Fairfax Resolves and wrote, in 1775, the Fairfax County Committee Resolutions. He agreed to serve on the Fairfax County Committee of Safety and consented to serve as a delegate to the Virginia Convention. He refused, however, to serve as a Member of the Continental Congress. He served in the Virginia Convention where he assumed a leadership role in drawing up the Declaration of Rights, and from 1777-1780 represented Fairfax County in the Virginia House of Delegates. His second marriage to Sarah Brent of Stafford County took place in 1780, and in 1781, then returning to home duties, he withdrew from the legislature.

Virginia still needed experienced leadership. Although he rejected efforts to persuade him to return to the General Assembly in 1784, he agreed to serve on the Virginia-Maryland Commission which was designed to settle questions concerning the Potomac River, 1784-1785. In 1786 he was again elected as a delegate from Fairfax to the General Assembly but did not attend the session. He agreed to accept appointment to the Virginia delegation which would attend the federal convention in Philadelphia, scheduled for convening in May, 1787, which was designed to consider revisions in the Articles of Confederation.

We now know, in retrospect, this meeting was to produce a new Constitution, a document which Mason would help shape. That story will be told elsewhere. However, it is appropriate to end this narrative of Mason's early career with a reference to his participation in the Virginia Convention, which, unforeseen by others, would provide the prelude for his successful championship of the Bill of Rights for inclusion in the U.S. Constitution.

Mason's political skill became evident in the work he accomplished on the drafting of the Virginia Declaration of Rights. We need to set the scene for this important work. The Continental Congress laid the road to independence for the colonies on May 10, 1776, when each state was requested to take action to assume sovereign powers. A first step in this role came with the establishment of a fundamental charter of government, a document which would lay out the preservation of the rights the settlers claimed as Englishmen, and which were now denied to them by their mother country. The easiest course was a modification of the colonial charter which outlined the fundamentals of government. Virginia possessed both the leadership and boldness to act. Five days later, the Virginia Convention followed the call of the Continental Congress by passing a resolution which created a committee to draw up a bill of rights and a constitution.

Mason would help shape this bill of rights and we can only speculate what would have happened if Mason had not consented to serve in the Virginia Convention: would the Virginia role been as important and essential in the absence of Mason? On the very question of the Declaration of Rights, one of Mason's biographer's Robert A. Rutland offers the perceptive observation:

> Few documents have ever had such a wide impact on society and yet brought so little public recognition for the principal author as the Virginia Declaration

of Rights.[14]

The Virginia Convention Committee faced an enormous task, working from experience and history to prepare a legal and political justification for the course the colonies were taking and to define a list of the essential rights to which they felt entitled. George Mason, probably because of his skill in expressing ideas into words, as well as his commitment to liberty, took the lead. Within the short span of four weeks, under Mason's leadership, the Virginia Convention had completed the formidable task: completed and reviewed two draft proposals, debated the theoretical and practical aspects of the crucial questions, and finally — by unanimous vote — adopted the Virginia Declaration of Rights.

During the critical week of May 20-26, Mason started with ten basic propositions. The Committee made eight additions to Mason's ideas. A draft copy was put in print by June 1, 1776. Concern among some of the delegates surfaced whether too broad a statement on the rights of individuals might be misinterpreted in a slave-owning society as advocating emancipation, and thus could encourage not only a movement for independence from Britain but a social revolution through an insurrection by the slaves.

The Convention debated the draft of the Declaration on June 3 and then turned to other matters until June 10. The debate ended on June 11, and with only one more session the Declaration won unanimous support.[15]

The final document, the Declaration of Rights, declared that all men are by nature "free and independent" and that they possess certain inherent rights such as "the enjoyment of life and liberty, with the means of acquiring and possessing property, and pursuing and obtaining happiness and safety."

This document viewed government as instituted for "the common benefit, protection, and security of the people, nation, or community ... " and that magistrates were the "trustees and servants" of the people and at all times "answerable" to them. It further noted that whenever government failed the purposes for which it had been created (e.g., producing the greatest degree of happiness and safety), then a majority of the community "hath an indubitable, unalienable, and indefeasible" right thus to "reform, alter, or abolish it" in any manner necessary beneficial for the people's welfare.[16]

The measure produced by the Virginia Convention further stated that the legislative and executive powers should be separate and distinct from the judicial ("Judicative") and that the legislative and executive members should be subject to frequent elections. A fundamental principle contained within it stated that those who are taxed or deprived of property should have given their consent to government to do so, and they should not be bound by any law to which they had not asserted through their representatives. Certain rights were listed as fundamental: the right to know of accusations in a capital or criminal prosecution, a speedy trial by an impartial jury, excessive bail should not be required, a person should not be compelled to give testimony against himself, general warrants for searches should not be allowed, freedom of the press should be secured and the press should not be restrained, a well regulated militia should be guaranteed, standing armies in time of peace should be avoided, and the military power should be subordinated to civil power.[17]

Finally, this charter for Virginians declared that no free government or the blessings of liberty could be preserved unless the people adhered to "justice, moderation, temperance, frugality, and virtue, and by frequent recurrence to fundamental principles." The final clause — No. 16 — declared religion could be directed only by "reason and convention, not by force and violence," and guaranteed the free exercise of religion according to the dictates of conscience.[18]

Though not credited by name, Mason's influence became enshrined in history in the acceptance by other colonies of Virginia's Declaration of Rights. The value of newspapers became evident as they spread the news of this amazing declaration. The *Virginia Gazette* had published a draft on

GEORGE MASON: THE PREPARATION FOR LEADERSHIP

June 1st and by June 6th, it appeared in the *Pennsylvania Evening Post*; a reprint appeared in June 8 and 12 in the *Pennsylvania Ledger* and *Pennsylvanian Gazette*. The *Maryland Gazette* reprinted it, and other newspapers did likewise, circulating up and down the coast within reach of the political leaders of each of the colonies. Pennsylvania took the lead and made the Virginia Declaration the model in seven states, as these states affixed a declaration of rights before the text of its constitution. Mason thus had made his mark on political history as Americans put in writing in their most fundamental document, a vision of the good society and asserted that the purpose of government was the protection of life, liberty, property, the pursuit of happiness, and the pursuit of safety.[19]

A reading of the Virginia Declaration of Rights, which emerged from Mason's hand, leaves little doubt of the great influence this document had on Thomas Jefferson when he authored the Declaration of Independence only a month later. This influence would be manifested again 11 years later when Mason pleaded for the inclusion of a list of rights in the new U.S. Constitution, and refused to sign the document because, among other reasons, it did not have a declaration of rights.

As we pause to review Mason's early career, we might ask where does George Mason stand when compared with his neighbors and the other Founding Fathers of the U.S. Constitution? The editor of his papers, Dr. Robert A. Rutland, presents this useful comparison of Mason with his contemporaries:

> Mason was a Virginian. Unquestionably, his Northern Neck origin was a controlling fact in his life. Mason's father and grandfather had been frontiersmen as well as gentlemen-planters. Father, son, and grandson had been born, raised and had died in a thirty-square-mile microcosm. Washington was an American, and then a Virginian. Jefferson was a man of the world, an American, and a Virginian. Madison

was a scholar, an American, and only incidentally a Virginian. In the company of the demigods, Mason was never ashamed to confess his primary allegiance to the colony and later the commonwealth of Virginia. But he also lacked Washington's vanity, Jefferson's dilettantism, and Madison's timidity on the slavery issue. At the right moment, this quartet of Virginians sensed a high obligation to all Americans, and this characteristic redeems their imperfections.[20]

Another biographer, Helen Hill Miller, has attempted to set Mason's role as in the shadow of these other Founding Fathers, not less significant but a victim of time and circumstances.

Down the years, George Mason's contributions to the constitution-making period, state and national, has been relatively little recognized. He died in 1792 at just the time when his chief colleagues became actors on the newly available national stage. He was just seven years older than Washington, who survived him by just that interval. He was older than Jefferson by eighteen years, than Madison by twenty-six, than Marshall by thirty, than Monroe by thirty-three. Because of his disappearance from the political scene at the moment of their emergence before the united country, their names survived while his tended to be lost to sight. But during the years from 1765 to 1789, he was in the forefront of Virginia's participation in great events, one of the chief political thinkers, draftsman, and negotiators who gave the new state, and later the new nation, its form.[21]

George Mason — father, planter, civic leader — emerged as a leader in Virginia government at a crucial time when his state was also contributing Washington, Jefferson, Madison, and Monroe. Though not prolific in writing, he left a legacy of thought which endured in the struggle for independence and in the period of constitution making, in the embodiment of a bill or declaration of rights by which government was instituted for the protection of its citizens. Mason desired a specific commitment by the citizens for a list of rights which no government could violate. As he wrote, spoke, conferred with colleagues, participated in governmental office, and reflected in the privacy of Gunston Hall Plantation, his quest for a specific declaration of rights in a government subjected to the control of the governed, was a legacy begun by Mason in the early years of his career — a quest which would assume dominant importance during the debate over the creation of U.S. Constitution and reaching fulfillment with the addition of the Bill of Rights as the first ten amendments to the Constitution. Mason left to his country and the world a legacy of constitutional liberty upholding individual rights.

Footnotes

1.   Robert A. Rutland, *George Mason: Reluctant Statesman*, Baton Rouge and London: Louisiana State University Press, 1961.
2.   Louis D. Rubin, Jr., *Virginia: A History*, New York : W. W. Norton and Company, 1984, pp. 4-7. One historian noted: "A chapter of Virginia history might well be given over to the career and achievements of John Rolfe, whose development of the first profitable export crop gave employment to shippers and merchants, stimulated transatlantic trade, and instilled a new spirit of confidence among the settlers." Matthew Page Andrews, *Virginia: The Old Dominion*, Richmond, Virginia, 1949, p. 69.
3.   Rubin, *Virginia: A History*, p. 14.
4.   *Ibid.*, pp. 32-36. A view of the Mason family through these different stages of Virginia history can be found in the work by Pamela C. Copeland and Richard K. MacMaster, *The Five George Masons: Patriots and Planters of Virginia and Maryland*, Charlottesville, Virginia, 1975.
5.   Robert E. and B. Katherine Brown, *Virginia 1705-1786: Democracy or Aristocracy*, East Lansing, Michigan: Michigan State University Press, 1964, pp. 3-5, 290-293, 307-308. The Browns move away from the class conflict theory — that the American revolution involved a split from Britain as well as an internal class revolution within American society — popularized by Carl L. Becker in *The History of Political Parties in the Province of New York, 1763-1776* (Madison, Wisconsin: University of Wisconsin Press, 1909) and Charles A. Beard in *An Economic Interpretation of the Constitution of the United States* (New York: Macmillan, 1941), first published in 1913. Brown acknowledges the work of Charles S. Sydnor, *Gentlemen Freeholders: Political Practices in Washington's Virginia* (Chapel Hill : University of North Carolina, 1952) who dismissed both the democratic and aristocratic elements in Virginia politics but Brown believes Sydnor gives undue greater stress to the aristocratic rather than democratic elements. An interesting interpretation of how Virginians were able to develop

republican institutions while maintaining slavery is found in Edmund S. Morgan, *American Slavery – American Freedom: The Ordeal of Colonial Virginia*, New York: W. W. Norton and Company, 1975.
6. Charles W. Stetson, *Washington and His Neighbors*, Richmond, Virginia: Garrett and Massie, 1956, pp. 199-201.
7. *Ibid.*, pp. 202-203.
8. *Ibid.*, pp. 204-205.
9. *Ibid.*, pp. 201, 205. This early history of the Mason family and plantation is covered by Helen Hill Miller, *George Mason: Gentleman Revolutionary*, Hill: The University of North Carolina Press, 1975, Chapters I-IV., pp. 3-87.
10. Robert A. Rutland, *George Mason and the War for American Independence*, Williamsburg, Virginia: Virginia Independence Bicentennial Commission, p. 23. The author observes that Mason owned about five thousand acres near Gunston Hall, had a good amount of cash, owned over one hundred slaves, and possessed shares in thousands of western acres. *Ibid*. Mason grieved for his wife and he wrote tenderly of her passing in the family Bible. He noted: "In the Beauty of her Person, & the Sweetness of her Disposition, she was equalled by few, & excelled by none of her Sex....Free from her Sex's smallest Faults, And fair as Woman-kind can be;" His full account can be found in the copy of the Mason family Bible in possession of Gunston Hall and in Appendix C of Robert A. Rutland (Editor), *The Papers of George Mason, 1725-1792*, Volume I, 1749-1778, Chapel Hill: The University of North Carolina Press, 1970, pp. 481-482.
11. Robert A. Rutland, Editor, *The Papers of George Mason, 1725-1792*, Volume I, 1749-1778, pp. cxiii-cxiv. References to what life was like at Gunston Hall can be found in the short collection by Joseph F. Anzenberger Jr. (Editor), *The Gunston Hall Collection of the Papers of George Mason*, a listing of the personal papers of George Mason located in the Gunston Hall Archives.
12. *Ibid.*, p. cxxvii. The editor provides a useful chronology of Mason's career in each of the three volumes of *The Papers of George Mason, 1725-1792*.
13. Rutland, *George Mason: Reluctant Statesman*, p. 25.
14. Rutland, *The Papers of George Mason, 1725-1792*, Volume 1, 1749-1778, p. 274. A number of works give an account of this period in Mason's life. See Irving Brant, *James Madison: The Virginia Revolutionist*, Indianapolis and New York: The Bobbs-Merrill Company, 1941; Helen Hill Miller, *George Mason: Gentleman Revolutionary*; and Lewis H. Machen, *George Mason of Virginia*, An address by Lewis H. Nachen presenting a portrait to Fairfax County, May 20, 1901, Press of Byron S. Adams, 1901. How this period related to the later influence of George Mason on the Bill of Rights can be examined in Robert A. Rutland, *The Birth of the Bill of Rights, 1776-1791*, Boston : Northeastern University Press, 1983 and T. Daniel Shumate, *The First Amendment: The Legacy of George Mason*, Fairfax, Virginia: George Mason University Press, 1987.
15. Rutland, *The Papers of George Mason, 1725-1792*, Volume 1, 1749-1778, pp. 274-275.
16. Virginia Declaration of Rights. The text can be found in many publications including *The Papers of George Mason, 1725-1792*, Volume 1, 1749-1778, pp. 276-278.
17. *Ibid*.
18. *Ibid*.
19. Rutland, *The Papers of George Mason, 1725-1792*, Volume I, 1749-1778, p. 276.
20. *Ibid.*, p. cxi. Although he does not give much attention to George Mason overall in his examination of Virginians' contribution to republican thought, historian Edmund Morgan cites the example of republican ideas by George Mason in his

exaltation of the militia and it prompted equality and freedom. Edmund Morgan, *American Slavery – American Freedom: The Ordeal of Colonial Virginia*, p. 379.

21. Miller, *George Mason: Gentleman Revolutionary*, Foreword. p. cxi. Two pamphlet surveys of the contributions of George Mason can be found in Helen Hill Miller, "George Mason: The Man Who Didn't Sign," Fairfax County, Virginia: The Board of Regents of Gunston Hall, 1987 and Donald J. Senese, "George Mason and the Bill of Rights," Fairfax County, Virginia: Fairfax County Bicentennial Commission, 1988.

GEORGE MASON AND THE FAIRFAX COURT

by Joseph Horrell

George Mason's admirers, described by one of them as a "small but avid band," owe a special debt to a handful of scholars who have kept his memory alive. The Founding Fathers left their own monument in the Constitution, but a grateful nation that celebrates its authors turns a blind eye to ghosts at the banquet. The older generation of revolutionaries who struck the spark that lit the fire in Virginia — in order of age, George Mason, Richard Henry Lee, Patrick Henry, and William Grayson — afterwards became Antifederalists, opposed ratification, uttered dire prophecies of the country's future, and lapsed into varying degrees of obscurity. George Mason spoke for all of them when he warned that an all-powerful central government "will only change the Name & place of Residence of our Tyrants."[1] It is a feat of historical scholarship that the cutting edge of his thought and words is felt today.

Not identified with high office but content to remain a country justice, the squire of Gunston Hall was fading from a public consciousness that venerated the Founding Fathers when in 1892 Kate Mason Rowland rescued him from oblivion. Because she drew on documents now lost, her two-volume biography is not likely to be superseded; but she does not lack able successors who have built on the foundations she laid. Now, with Robert Rutland's magisterial three-volume edition of Mason's public and private papers, the present generation is privileged to gain the acquaintance of Washington's friend and mentor in constitutional matters, a statesman ranked by Jefferson as "of the first order of greatness," whose conversation Madison described simply as "a feast." As much new light, however, as Rowland's successors have shed upon various aspects of Mason's career, they have left his service on the Fairfax County Court obscure and (in the telling) confused.

Rowland wrote a long chapter on George Mason's formative years, 1725-64, without mentioning the Fairfax court at all.[2] Her successors fill the void, but read the record of his service variously; some misread it; and all put the emphasis in the wrong place.[3] Rutland states that Mason was first named to the Fairfax court, "a demanding and important office," in the decade following his defeat in the burgesses' election of 1748.[4] The fact that these events took place in the reverse order is less important than Rutland's view that Mason's service as a justice was a shaping influence on his life and thought. He puts it this way:

> A different course of legal training for Mason was given by the county court. Before he was thirty the young planter began serving as a justice of the peace in Fairfax County. This was the most important of the local appointive offices a gentleman might hold, for it was practically a lifetime job with a broad range of duties. Not only did the justice settle minor suits, issue peace bonds, and send out court orders; he also sat with the other justices of the county in the important monthly "court days." The whole spectrum of civil and criminal cases passed before the assembled justices.[5]

The record of Mason's service, as preserved mainly in 4,000 folio-size manuscript pages of the surviving Fairfax County Court minutes during his lifetime, does not support this or any other current interpretation.[6]

Upon attaining his majority at the end of 1746, George Mason took legal possession of one of the largest estates in Fairfax County.[7] His accession to rank as a gentleman justice, vestryman, and militia officer was virtually foreordained. Early in his twenty-first year, he was named to the commission of the peace for Fairfax County (22 April 1747),[8] and his election to the Truro vestry and commissioning in the county militia followed in due course. He had been born into the county oligarchy.[9] Election to the House of Burgesses was somewhat more problematical because the quorum of senior justices, defined as the upper half of the commission, usually supplied four candidates for the two seats.[10] Mason failed on his first poll in 1748 but was elected in 1758.

By inheritance Mason belonged to the privileged class of gentlemen justices who were expected to assemble at the courthouse once a month to govern the county and decide lawsuits without compensation of any kind except prestige. For the court to sit, the law required that at least one member of the quorum and three additional justices be present. In Fairfax County the monthly sessions of one to five days used up thirty to forty days a year. Owing to the heavy demands on their time, the senior justices spelled each other at presiding, and on routine court days from four to eight justices generally occupied the Fairfax bench, seated in strict order of seniority starting with the "judge's chair." The court habitually adjourned one day to reconvene the next morning at nine o'clock (except for adjournment "until the court in course"). When days were short a sitting might last into candlelight. Duties were burdensome for all the justices, not least for Mason. Of the large estates in Fairfax County his was farthest from the courthouse, whether in its original location or at Alexandria. His patrimony of the lowest Tidewater neck in the county was a good three-hour ride away. The trip to the House of Burgesses in Williamsburg rarely took less than five days. Good health and a strong constitution were almost indispensable for public service in colonial times, and Mason had neither.[11]

The court to which Mason was named was barely five years old. At the creation of Fairfax County out of Prince William in 1742, the original commission was headed by William Fairfax, Lord Fairfax's kinsman and representative for the Northern Neck land office, who promptly got himself elected a burgess for the new county as he had been for the old. A number of the justices, including Lewis Ellzey, the original sheriff, had earlier sat on the Prince William bench.

Upon William Fairfax's elevation to the Council in 1744, John Colvill moved to the judge's chair which, as well as being elected a burgess, he occupied until his death in 1756. During this period, owing to the deaths of Richard Osborn, one of the Fairfax burgesses, and Jeremiah Bronaugh, Mason's uncle, Ellzey rose to second place and generally alternated with Colvill as presiding justice; he was to serve the court longer (until 1770) than any other of its original members. Two other justices whose appointments in 1745 antedated Mason's — George William Fairfax and John West — were also to give long and faithful service in the judge's chair. Daniel McCarty, Mason's friend and neighbor at Cedar Grove, and Charles Broadwater of Springfield, both junior to Mason in rank, assiduously attended and often presided. The court minutes clearly demonstrate that all the justices mentioned attended faithfully year in and year out except Mason.[12]

Whatever their versions of Mason's experience as a justice, his biographers unanimously overlook the fact that he was dropped from the commission dated 30 April 1752.[13] The minutes, complete for the preceding three years, show that during these thirty-six months the court sat for a total of fifty-seven days and that Mason attended three full days and part of a fourth. No other justice surpassed his record of nonattendance. He did not sit at all in 1750, and his one day in 1751 came too early for him to qualify under a new commission later in the year. After being dropped he was not named to the commission for twelve years. If the Fairfax court provided a course for Mason's early training, he chiefly distinguished himself by skipping classes. Precious few cases, let alone a spectrum, passed before Mason at this or any other time.

The circumstances surrounding Mason's removal indicate pretty clearly that it came as a surprise. In January the court had ordered the erection in Alexandria of whipping post, stocks, and ducking pool in anticipation of the court's relocation from its original upcountry site (on land deeded to its use by William Fairfax), to the burgeoning port town of which Lord Fairfax and other Fairfax connections were original trustees. The relocation was approved by the Council, headed by William Fairfax, on 25 April. The preceding month Mason had taken title to three lots in the new county town.¹⁴ A number of justices were to justify the expense of a *pied-à-terre* in Alexandria because it relieved them from daily rides to courts as well as from nights spent with the mixed company and rations of ordinaries.

Other circumstances involve larger issues. By coincidence Mason was first named to the Fairfax court at a moment when the Council was scrutinizing the commissions of the peace throughout the colony. In their judicial incarnation as the General Court, the councillors employed their executive power to ferret out the reason for delays in the county courts. They soon satisfied themselves that the blame lay with justices who made small return in attendance for the prestige they enjoyed on or off the bench. In 1748 they ordered the clerks of the courts to report within six months of receiving a new commission "the Names of those Gentlemen appointed Justices who refuse to Qualify themselves as such."¹⁵ Two years later they advertised this order in the gazettes and added a second which decreed that if a justice did not appear in court to take the oaths within six months after a new commission was received, the court should not qualify him.¹⁶ Another two years passed, and the Council again found it necessary to place on its agenda with Governor Dinwiddie "the Delay of Justice in the County Courts." Up to this time the Council had generally complied with recommendations by the courts for additions until many of the commissions, including the one for Fairfax, had grown to a score of justices. Now Dinwiddie and his lieutenants decided that the blame lay in "the too great Number and Neglect of Justices." Preliminary to taking action, the Council ordered all the court clerks to "attend the Governor on the 25th of April Next [1752] with a List of the Justices who have Qualify'd themselves, of those who have refused, and their Reasons for such Refusal."¹⁷ From every corner of the colony the clerks descended on the capital. There were almost fifty of them.

Before most of the clerks could return home the Governor and Council swung the axe. On 30 April — only five days after relocation of the Fairfax courthouse — they issued new commissions for forty-four counties arranged from Accomac to York (Dinwiddie and Halifax had been provided for on 22 April).[18] Commissions that had expanded to a score of justices were cut in half. The victims ranged from justices of long standing to young men whose appointments the Governor and Council had approved in the past two years, some only months earlier. The Fairfax commission was reduced from twenty-two to ten; Mason was among the dozen purged.[19]

By this ukase, which departed from traditional practice, the Governor and Council depopulated upwards of a third of the colony's precincts of peace officers. In the same degree they created a surplus of constables who could find no magistrate within reach to sign precepts for detaining suspects for a hearing at the next court. In the shorn Fairfax commission Anthony Russell of Cameron Parish, who lived thirty miles from the new courthouse, found himself the sole magistrate for an area that five years later became Loudoun County with thirteen justices. As recommendations streamed in for appointment of new justices and reappointment of old, the Governor and Council steadily gave ground. In 1758, tempered by experience, the Council requested county clerks to specify "the Place where Gentlemen recommended to be added to the Commission reside."[20] Within five years of its purge the Fairfax court rose to eighteen justices and by 1761 to twenty-three.[21] Mason was not among those who wished to exchange the frowns of power for smiles. He enjoyed a militia commission as colonel and served in the House, 1758-61, but showed no disposition to rejoin the court.

While absent, Mason witnessed from the vantage of the House a local controversy which was to persist in his memory hardly less than the purge. In 1759 discontented freeholders of Fairfax County openly challenged the court's authority in a matter of taxation. The justices had levied a tax of 22,000 pounds of tobacco on the county's tithables to build a tobacco wharf in Alexandria. Patently, a disproportionate share of the tax would be paid by planters with many tithables, and a disproportionate benefit would accrue to Alexandria merchants with few. The unhappy taxpayers petitioned the House of Burgesses that the justices who levied the tax be required by law to repay the quantity of tobacco to the county.[22] The House referred the matter to the Committee on Propositions and Grievances. This body concluded that the justices should refund the full amount and collect the same from the trustees of Alexandria out of wharfage. After two readings, a bill to this effect was referred to George Johnston, one of the Fairfax burgesses (Mason being the other), who made several amendments. The amended bill was read a third time and put to a vote only to be rejected.[23] The unhappy Fairfax taxpayers lost their tobacco but retained their grievance against a court which appeared to them unduly influenced by Alexandria merchants. The groundwork had been laid, apparently without much help from Mason, for his subsequent role as champion of the "country" party.

Mason could have returned to the Fairfax commission at any time he chose, and the reason for his abstention is not clear. Perhaps he excused himself from an uncongenial task because of other preoccupations. Since his appointment in 1751 as treasurer of the Ohio Company, much of his time was absorbed by the troubled and uncertain affairs of this speculative venture, whose fate would perhaps be determined by the war. His protracted absence from the Fairfax court spanned the entire seven-year-long war between Britain and France for dominion in North America. The burning issue of the time was the security of Virginia's frontiers and the expulsion of the French from her vast transmontane territory, in which dozens of speculators had staked out claims. Mason's friend and neighbor at Mount Vernon, Colonel Washington, came into colonywide prominence as a soldier while Mason performed obscure legislative tasks in support of the war. Britain's triumphant peace revived dreams of new settlements and huge profits on the Ohio — there was even talk of a fourteenth colony; but the Proclamation of 1763 shocked Virginians out of their dreams. George III honored Britain's wartime agreement with the Indians to leave them in undisturbed possession of their hunting grounds in return for their deserting the French. Colonial governors could not make new grants or honor old ones for lands west of the Alleghenies. Had the king violated Virginia's ancient charters?

Although Mason recognized immediately that the proclamation spelled the destruction of the Ohio Company's grant, it was not until after the Revolution that he openly described the king's action as "absolutely illegal & void."[24] If he held this view in 1763, as almost certainly he did, it must have been reinforced by the Sugar Act of 1764 and the Stamp Act of 1765. He moved steadily from humble and deferential petitioner for property claims to peremptory spokesman for the legal and constitutional rights of a nation. His biographers from Kate Mason Rowland onward have recognized 1764 as a pivotal year when he shifted from a passive to an active role in the colony's affairs. But not having observed his dismissal, they have overlooked the fact that this was also the year when, not holding any other political office, he chose to rejoin the Fairfax court. Save the Truro vestry, on which he served for thirty-six years, this was to prove the only office he held on to for the rest of his public career.

Mason reappeared in the commission of twenty-four justices recorded at Fairfax court on 21 November 1764.[25] Because seniority was reckoned from date of earliest service, he was named in fourth place, just ahead of Daniel McCarty, as before, and after George William Fairfax, Lewis Ellzey, and John West; his absence had not cost him his seniority. By 1770, owing to Fairfax's elevation to the Council and Ellzey's retirement, Mason had risen to second place, with John West occupying the judge's chair.[26] His appointment to successive commissions suggests that he appeared often enough to qualify, but the surviving court minutes, complete from 15 August 1768 to 22 February 1774, show that his attendance was negligible. Out of 183 court days, he sat only 4 entire days and another 14 partial days, and in almost every case these were days when he had private business in court. Before rejoining the court, he had sold the last of his properties in Alexandria. By this time he was assailed by a multitude of ailments, chronic or acute, chiefly "wandering gout" and "convulsive cholic," which often reduced him to transport by sedan chair or support by crutches and which limited his mobility for the rest of his life. His colleagues spared him the physical exertion of serving in the office of sheriff, which rotated among the senior justices; Daniel McCarty served two one-year terms, Charles Broadwater four; Mason never. His temperamental dislike of public bodies had found a constitutional ally.

But his ailments relaxed their grip during the crisis that culminated in independence. He pushed resistance efforts against the Stamp Act, 1765-66; helped shape the nonimportation agreements, 1769; researched Virginia's charters, 1773; contributed to the Fairfax Resolves and helped organize the independent Fairfax militia company, 1774. When Washington left Virginia to take command of the Continental forces in 1775, Mason was spurred to renewed efforts both in Fairfax County and in the Virginia Convention, 1775-76. His epoch-making drafts of the Declaration of Rights and the Virginia constitution were adopted almost as written, and (though he had refused a seat in the Continental Congress) he represented Fairfax County in the General Assembly of the new commonwealth of his design, 1777-81. Much of the voluminous legislation urgently passed to support Washington's army and the war bore the mark of his pen. The prodigious amount of work turned out by this semi-invalid and hypochondriac would have exceeded the physical and intellectual capacity of most of his contemporaries. After Yorktown made the outcome certain, Mason once more succumbed to his illnesses and did not revive until the Federal and ratification conventions loomed.

In shaping a plan of government for the Commonwealth of Virginia, Mason emasculated the Council by transferring its legislative authority to an elective senate and its judicial to independent superior courts. He reduced it, as Madison said, to "a grave of useful talents." But Mason had no more to say about the commission of the peace than the solitary sentence, "Let the Governour, and Privy Council, appoint justices of the peace for the counties."[27] This was obviously insufficient, and in the final draft hands unknown struck out all of Mason's hortatory subjunctives in favor of imperatives and added a clause: "The Governour, with the advice of the Privy Council, shall appoint Justices of the Peace for the counties; and in case of vacancies, or a necessity of increasing the number hereafter, such appointments to be made upon the recommendation of the respective county courts."[28] In thus denying Governor and Council, by omission, any right to fill vacancies or to establish commissions *de novo*, the constitution eliminated an objectionable, if rarely used, prerogative of the royal government without providing that the county courts should function any differently under the republican. Mason soon came to realize that in their authority to nominate their members the county courts enjoyed "a Power unknown in any other Part of the Constitution."[29]

These concessions to the county courts at the expense of Whig principles were in sharp contrast to the popular sovereignty which Mason breathed from his bill of rights into every other department of government. On the one hand, the bill of rights asserted that the people could not be taxed (i.e., deprived of their property) without their consent or the consent of their elected representatives. On the other, the constitution countenanced in county government an age-old institution, self-perpetuating, nonelective, and for all practical purposes hereditary in Virginia (in most respects, the old royal Council writ small) wherein a conflict between new principle and old practice must arise every time such a body set the county levy, which it did once a year. Constitutional questions that had agitated the best minds of the time were destined to arise in county courts throughout Virginia to confuse country justices, few of whom had any formal training in the law. Indeed, these issues plagued the father of Virginia's constitution till the end of his life.

Upon the death of Colonel West in 1777, Mason succeeded to the judge's chair. His appearances remained as infrequent as ever; he happily yielded the chair to his diligent friend Daniel McCarty. In 1780, however, an issue arose that stirred his interest. In addition to the regular annual levy the sitting justices imposed and collected 30,000 pounds of tobacco "unapplied to any particular Use or Purpose," but (according to Mason) "with a View of future Application to the Emolument of the Town." Mason remembered the celebrated case of the Alexandria wharf which occurred when he was absent from the commission. Now he was chief judge, but he obviously had not been present to prevent the abuse complained of. He blamed the "Town Justices," who, "being always upon the Spot," were able "to avail themselves of the Absence of the Country Members."[30]

Faced with an accomplished fact, the country justices mustered sufficient strength to prevent any subsequent annual levies being laid until the tobacco surplus was used up. But the aftermath was "Party-feuds" such that "the Decisions of some of the Justices will depend more upon the Name or Place of Residence of the Plaintif or Defendant, than upon the Merits of the Cause." The moving force behind the delayed and acrimonious reaction of the country justices was George Mason. He stopped short of denying the court's right to levy any tax whatever — but not far short.

Two years later he launched a public attack on the county courts. This took the form of a petition dated 8 June 1782 and addressed to the Speaker and gentlemen of the House of Delegates, with ninety-seven signatories of Fairfax County including Mason. The petitioners protested that the power exercised by the justices of the county courts in:

> levying unlimited Sums of Tobacco or Money upon the People, is not only inconsistent with the fundamental Principles of a free Government, but expressly contrary to the Spirit and Letter of our own Bill of Rights; which declares that the People shall not, "be taxed or deprived of their Property

for public Uses, without their own Consent, or that of their Representatives.["]

The county court was criticized as an unrepresentative body, self-contained and perpetuated by its own recommendation of members. Its decisions were subject to party and faction, which had the effect of "prostituting it to the Purposes of private Interest, or personal Malice," so that "from a Court so constituted common Justice is hardly to be expected." Mason ruefully conceded that the justices were appointed in the manner prescribed by "a very faulty Part of our Constitution," which everyone knew he wrote. The petition rambled over an accumulation of grievances (including the one of 1780), some specific, some general, accusing an unnamed justice of acting in one instance "with a Degree of Insolence & Partiality that disgraced the Bench." Mason left no doubt in anyone's mind that it was the Alexandria faction that furnished the flagrant example.[31]

In this context of indignation the proposed remedies seem very modest: A law should exclude borough officials from the county court; the same law should set an upper limit on the levy not to be exceeded without approval of freeholders or their representatives. The provision in the constitution for nominating justices, however defective, could not be altered until a convention for such express purposes was elected. For the moment the proposed legislative remedy had to suffice. The courthouse and prison should not be removed from Alexandria at that time, as other petitioners proposed, because recent repairs assured "many Years" of service, and with wartime prices the expense could not be justified.[32]

Not surprisingly, the town justices in a counterpetition of 20 November 1782 decried this "illiberal" and "unmanly" attack on their characters "with a pen dip'd in Gall" by a supposed author "Notorious for his non-attendance at Court."[33] They made the telling point that they were nominated by the procedure laid down in the constitution. Was their assailant ignorant of this document? But their demand for the constitutional right accorded even "the greatest of Criminals" to confront their accusers fell on deaf ears. The General Assembly chose to sidestep this local quarrel.

The next year Mason took another slap at the Fairfax court. On 22 October 1783 he occupied the judge's chair briefly before surrendering it to Daniel McCarty when the crier called the suit of Hooe and Harrison and Company against George Mason, Gentleman, in trespass on the case. By their attorney, the plaintiffs claimed £150 in damages for a consignment of goods that Mason seems to have rejected because it was in improper condition or incomplete. Appearing for himself, Mason produced a writ of *certiorari*, and the justices ordered the case to be transferred to the General Court. The formal deposition which Mason had submitted in support of his writ alleged that several of the justices likely to hear his case were merchants and shipowners, who could not be impartial. Furthermore, trial juries were drawn from the same class of Alexandria citizens. This might have been sufficient, but Mason proceeded to rake over the coals of old controversies. He charged that the town justices had conceived a prejudice against him when he threatened to expose by an "information" to the Governor and Council their unwarranted levying of 30,000 pounds of tobacco upon the people "for no certain or avowed purpose whatsoever." He also incurred their dislike by seeking their exclusion from the county court, for all of which "he hath good reasons to believe he hath very little chance for common justice in the said County Court of Fairfax."[34] Mason resumed the chair, sat through the remainder of the day, signed the minutes, and went home. This was his second and last appearance for the year.

On 22 March 1785 Mason returned to the attack, but this time he aimed his fire at the Governor and Council. The previous 25 October Gov. Benjamin Harrison, as one of the last acts of his term, had acceded to the Council's advice and issued new commissions of the peace for Virginia counties. All persons in former commissions were named except those who had died, resigned, moved out of the county, or refused or neglected to qualify within twelve months after being named.[35] This seeming usurpation of the justices' right to nominate their members was bound to stir memories of the great purge of 1752. Only two from that era still sat on the Fairfax bench, Charles Broadwater, who had survived the purge, and George Mason, one of its victims. They and other justices appear to have arranged with the clerk not to bring the new commission to the court's official notice until they were ready with a protest.

The presence of ten justices at the courthouse on 22 March, particularly the chief judge, although he arrived late, presaged something extraordinary. After Mason took the judge's chair, the court ordered the clerk to record a protest in which the justices "unanimously" refused to receive the new commission.[36] The clerk was further ordered to send a copy to the executive — by this time Patrick Henry — from whom Mason could expect a sympathetic hearing.

The arguments for refusing to accept the commission were familiar ones drawn from the bill of rights and the constitution. Mason denied the right of Governor and Council to appoint former or acting justices *de novo* (this implying the right to vacate commissions) or to dismiss any justice, "both of which it is notorious were frequently practiced under the former Government." Although willing to absolve Governor and Council of "evil Purposes" — a concession rare in Mason's polemics — the protest took the view that accepting "such a Commission wou'd afford a dangerous precedent, and tend to renew in this Commonwealth, one of the many abuses & arbitrary practices of the late monarchical Government here." The Fairfax court continued to sit under the previous commission, absent Mason as usual.

Up to now Mason's politics in Fairfax County had been divisive; but with the conventions of 1787 and 1788 they turned schismatic. During the four months of debate in Philadelphia presided over by George Washington, Mason appeared for the first and last time on the national stage, where the old revolutionary proved himself "able and convincing in debate, steady and firm in his principles, and undoubtedly one of the best politicians in America" — but not without offense to his constituents.[37] After the Constitution emerged from the delegates' protracted labors, incorporating many of Mason's views, he refused to sign because (at the head of his list of "Objections") it lacked a bill of rights. His widely circulated "Objections" became a rallying point for Antifederalists in Virginia and elsewhere. Washington believed that Mason had rendered himself "obnoxious" in Philadelphia and that his conduct "is not less reprobated in this County" (Fairfax). Madison wrote Jefferson in Paris that "his conduct has given great umbrage to the County of Fairfax, and particularly to the Town of Alexandria."[38]

After recovering from his trip to Philadelphia, Mason transferred the scene of political battle with the Alexandria merchants to Richmond. There, in the last session of the General Assembly that he was to attend, commencing 26 October 1787, he secured the passage of an act that denied borough officials (members of a corporation court, court of hustings, or common council) the right to sit on a county court, limited the jurisdiction of borough courts to borough residents, and prohibited borough residents who enjoyed representation from also voting in county elections.[39] This was as much as he could do short of putting the seal on the schism by moving the courthouse out of Alexandria.

Although Mason, gout and colic notwithstanding, was determined to attend the ratifying convention in Richmond, for a time any chance of his being elected a delegate seemed foreclosed. As in all elections, the poll would be taken at the courthouse, and Alexandria was arrayed in solid phalanx against him. To prove Mason's hostility to the town's citizens, Robert T. Hooe, one of the town justices Mason had belabored, paid the *Virginia Journal and Alexandria Advertiser* to print Mason's deposition of 1783 in six successive issues "Word for Word."[40] The situation was not much more favorable in the county. Every Fairfax freeholder knew that the victorious general at Mount Vernon, silent in public because of the certainty that a grateful nation would choose him as its first president under the proposed Constitution, favored ratification and an end to the seemingly endless debate. Mason's political problem was acute. If he somehow managed to get elected in Fairfax County, he was certain to be "tied up by express instructions"; the greater likelihood was that the freeholders would not send him to Richmond.[41] He arranged to be petitioned to offer himself in Stafford County, campaigned with unwonted vigor, and narrowly gained election; he then went to Richmond for the bitterest defeat of his career. Virginia ratified — just barely. A switch of five votes would have changed the outcome.

Sooner or later Virginia's ratification was bound to confront her leading Antifederalists with a crisis. Article VI of the newly engrossed document provided that all legislators and all executive and judicial officers "both of the United States and of the several States, shall be bound by Oath or Affirmation, to support this Constitution." In the House of Delegates, where he reigned with a clear Antifederalist majority, Patrick Henry declared his aversion to the Constitution so great that he would not take the oath. His refusal to contest for a seat in the United States Senate was ascribed to his nonjuroring; but he engineered the election of two fellow Antifederalists, Richard Henry Lee and William Grayson, whose consciences were less tender.[42] For George Mason, who aspired to no office he did not already hold, the crisis was deferred.

Mason professed as early as 1783 to have retired from public life, "yet my Anxiety for my Country, in these Times of Danger, makes me sometimes dabble a little in Politicks."[43] His biographers have regarded his defeat in Richmond, following close upon the one in Philadelphia, as marking the close of his public career. But upon either Mason's authority or theirs this makes an unwarranted exception of the Fairfax court. Up to his neck in county politics, Mason showed no disposition to resign his rightful place as presiding justice, even if he rarely presided. When he returned in ill-humor to Gunston Hall in July 1788, he no longer had a faithful surrogate in Daniel McCarty, who had resigned in 1784, but the country party he headed still enjoyed the support of the justice next in seniority, Charles Broadwater, and of younger men like Martin Cockburn and Richard Chichester. Despite the local following he had sacrificed in opposing ratification, he could still muster a majority of freeholders and fellow justices on county-versus-town issues, and no one could match the influence he wielded among his erstwhile colleagues in the General Assembly.

Mason did not attend the Fairfax court during all 1788, but towards the end of the year, on 16 December, the minutes touched a nerve:

> Ordered that the Sheriff [Robert T. Hooe] give notice that application will be made to the next Court to levy Tobacco for either building a new Court House or repairing the present one, and request that a general meeting of the Justices of the said County may be at the next Court.

Despite infrequent sittings and poor attendance in winter months, on 19 January 1789, the first day of the session, Mason's faction was strongly represented in the twenty justices who appeared. Even so, he must have recognized that he lacked the needed votes, for as presiding justice, he adjourned the court to meet the following day at eleven o'clock, two hours later than the customary time. On 20 January with Mason arriving late, the muster showed the unheard-of number of twenty-two. A headcount apparently convinced him he could now safely proceed. The first of his twin maneuvers to separate the courthouse from Alexandria is clear from the minutes:

> On a motion for levying Tobacco to erect a new Courthouse or repair the present one, it was objected that the Court had no legal authority to levy on the inhabitants of the county any money or Tobacco for any purpose whatever, and the question being put whether they were vested with that power

or not, George Mason, Charles Broadwater, Martin Cockburn, Richard Chichester, David Arell, Charles Little, William Payne, Charles Alexander, Roger West, William Lyles, William Herbert and Thomas Gunnell, Gentlemen were of opinion that power was taken from the County Courts by the bill of rights of this Commonwealth, and Robert Adam, George Gilpin, John Moss, David Stuart, James Wren, Richard Conway, John Fitzgerald, William Brown, Benjamin Dulaney and John Potts Gentlemen were of contrary opinion.[44]

A remonstrance against levying Tobacco or money for the purpose of building or repairing a Courthouse in the town of Alexandria signed by a number inhabitants of this County was produced in Court and read, which is ordered to be Certified [i.e., to be sent to the General Assembly].

George Mason did not sign the minutes as presiding justice, which suggests that he left as soon as his business was completed. The courthouse in Alexandria, falling into ruin, was not to be repaired. The justices would have to find another habitation.

By a majority of two, the justices had put on record their strict construction of the Whig principles of their leader, but as a practical matter, they appear to have followed him up a blind alley. What was to be done about the annual levy? Without it, there would be no provision for paying the county's only salaried officials, the sheriff, clerk, and commonwealth's attorney, besides incidental fees due them and the gaoler, constables, sheriff's deputies, coroners, and the like. Retiring to Gunston Hall, the chief judge abandoned this troublesome detail to his colleagues.

In his absence, with the business of the annual levy already past due, they ordered the clerk to dispatch a copy of the minutes of 20 January, denying the motion to levy taxes, to the Council for advice and to the attorney general for a legal opinion. On 3 February the Council referred the matter to the attorney general and on 12 February ordered that his decision be transmitted to the clerk of Fairfax County. Though the text of his opinion has not been found, the attorney general presumably affirmed the right to lay levies and emboldened the justices to reverse themselves.[45] On 17 February,

> the Court having reconsidered their power in laying levies for the use of the County, Charles Broadwater, Charles Little, John Moss, William Payne, Charles Alexander, William Brown, William Lyles, Richard Conway, and William Herbert were of opinion that they had a right to levy, to which opinion Roger West dissented.

Having reconsidered, they then proceeded to lay the levy. Mason thus lost on 17 February seven of the votes which had supported his position of 20 January — but had he? The silence of the levy regarding funds for the courthouse indicated that, for the moment at least, Mason had carried the essential point. And he was not done.

Mason next drafted a petition to build a new courthouse in a central location, secured 558 signatures (a clear majority in Fairfax County), and lobbied members of the General Assembly when it was presented on 3 November. The petition, in Mason's usual aggressive style of polemic, charged that the present location, "within Two hundred Yards of the Boundary of the State of Virginia," compelled the people to spend their money in tippling houses and taverns, discouraged country justices from attending, and left jury service to townsmen of little property, foreigners, and strangers, "whereby the Administration of Justice is Rendered precarious and capricious, and Property as well as Liberty unsafe."[46] The town party could muster only 109 names to a counterpetition presented on 12 November. Their reply to the "unbounded calumny" of Mason's petition was unavailing. The Committee on Propositions and Grievances decided in his favor. The "Act for altering the place of holding courts in the county of Fairfax" passed on 4 December 1789.[47] Unavoidable delays in finding the present site gave the Alexandrians time to petition for repeal of the act, but Mason was relentless. In a second petition, he berated the town justices for obstructing the will of the General Assembly and accused them of collecting the names of sailors and other itinerants, some fictitious, for their memorial.[48] Second only to Gunston Hall, the present-day courthouse of Fairfax County is a monument to George Mason. Rarely has the location of a mere edifice evoked so much Whig vehemence of purest strain.

Before he had secured the relocation, Mason formally brought his public career to a close where it had begun — in the Fairfax court. Preserved in the matter-of-fact tone of the minutes, this episode is in its own way dramatic; perhaps it should also be described as obscure, because by overlooking it Rutland failed to add Mason's letter of resignation to his *Papers*. The political background is sufficiently clear by now. The personal background for the scene in Fairfax court is provided by Mason's letter to his son John on 15 March 1789, just after Washington had become the first president under the Constitution:

> You know the friendship which has long existed (indeed from our early youth) between General Washington and myself. I believe there are few men in whom he placed greater confidence; but it is possible my opposition to the new government, both as a member of the national and of the Virginia Convention, may have altered the case. In this important trust, I am truly conscious of having acted from the purest motives of honesty, and love to my country, according to that measure of judgment which God has bestowed on me, and I would not forfeit the approbation of my own mind for the approbation of any man, or all the men upon earth.[49]

Mason's poignancy was genuine. The breach between Washington and Mason was one of the saddest consequences of the great struggle to which each lent his unique talents. But Mason's defiance was no less genuine and certainly characteristic.

On 17 August 1789 the Fairfax court assembled, absent Mason as usual, on the first day of its monthly session. With Charles Broadwater in the judges's chair, the eleven gentlemen justices present,

> agreeable to an act of the Congress of the United States intitled "An act to regulate the time and manner of administering certain Oaths," solemnly made Oath that they would support the Constitution of the United States.

After the justices, the oath was taken by the sheriff (Robert T. Hooe) and his deputies (Baldwin Dade and Jesse Moore), by the clerk of the court (Peter Wagener) and his deputy (George Deneale), and by the commonwealth's attorney (Bushrod Washington). The semiannual grand jury was routinely sworn. Then the clerk entered a minute more detailed than any comparable one in the history of the court:

> George Mason Gentn having signified his resignation of the Office of a Magistrate for this County by Letter, the same is ordered to be recorded and is in these words to wit, "Gunston Hall July 20th 1789. Gentlemen, as I do not intend to continue in the Office of a Magistrate or Justice of the Peace in Fairfax County, I do hereby resign the said Office and desire that this my resignation of the same may be entered of Record, that I may not be subjected to censure for refusing to execute the Dutys of an office which I no longer hold. I am, with much respect, your Worship's most obdt Servt G. Mason. To the Worshipful the Justices of Fairfax County Court."[50]

For all the ambiguity of Mason's letter, its political context leaves little doubt as to where he stood. The compliance of his colleagues, whether his fellow Antifederalists or the Fairfax justices, did not sway him. He had professed to oppose ratification because the Constitution lacked, among other things, a bill of rights. By resigning he avoided refusal to swear allegiance to a Constitution he opposed. Even if his health and disposition had permitted, he could not have accepted the commission that Gov. Beverley Randolph and the Council sent him in 1790 to fill the vacancy in the United States Senate created by Grayson's death. His nonjuroring made his isolation complete. His death in 1792 went virtually unnoticed.

In spite of all his excoriations of the Fairfax court, Mason viewed the venerable institution it represented with a divided mind. Willing to concede that justices were selected by an "unfortunate, and ill-judged Clause in our Constitution,"[51] he seemed never to find the time to repair the defect. On 6 May 1783 he wrote Patrick Henry that it was too soon after the war to elect delegates to a convention for revising the Virginia Constitution, and he firmly opposed on principle the idea of the General Assembly dissolving itself into a convention without elections for that purpose.[52] Later in the year Madison wrote Jefferson that in a visit to Gunston Hall, he had found Mason "sound and ripe" for reform, but he read only one side of Mason's mind.[53] In any event it was Jefferson the rationalist, not Mason the traditionalist, who in 1785 promoted legislation that among other reforms would at least have made the county courts elective. A stone wall of opposition defeated this least radical of Jefferson's reforms.[54] The legislators in Richmond, many of them country justices themselves, proved as reluctant as Mason to tamper with the foundation stone of government.

Attractive to him as the idea might have been on constitutional grounds, Mason recoiled from trying to reduce this least common denominator by separating its executive, legislative, and judicial functions, or even by providing for popular election of its members. He spared himself no fatigue or discomfort in promoting these cardinal principles in state and national government, where he did not intend to serve. He was querulous close to home, where he was the fourth George Mason to head the court of his county of residence. The Fairfax court, no matter how far short of theoretical perfection it fell, could be kept in check by vigilant freeholders, particularly those like himself willing to "dabble a little in Politicks," With his fear of "speculative theoretical Projects," Mason clung to the heritage of "our ancestors." "Uninterrupted life & long Experience," he wrote in another connection, "carry with them a Conviction of general Utility."[55] The venerable institution of the commission of the peace, transplanted from England to the American wilderness, was left in Virginia virtually undisturbed by the Revolution.[56] Besides the common law, it was the mother country's most cherished — and least feared — gift.

Since George Mason was in every public office a "reluctant statesman," as Rutland aptly describes him, why did he cling so long to the judge's chair he so rarely occupied? From the rich store of his papers there is no easy answer to be tapped, but they are so eloquent of his education and temperament that one may be distilled. He always had in his mind's eye "that once glorious and happy commonwealth" the Roman republic. He inscribed on the great seal of the Commonwealth of Virginia "Virtus ... dressed like an Amazon ... treading on Tyranny," with Libertas, Ceres, and Aeternitas on the obverse. He concluded his Declaration of Rights by exhorting his fellow Virginians to adhere to justice, moderation, temperance, frugality, and virtue. His words glow with his conviction that Roman virtues are "the vital principle of a republic." But the glow lights the shadow in which all of Virginia's great Antifederalists stand.

In Mason's mind, his Romans reached "their meredian glory" at the time of the first Punic War, when Rome could be compared in area and population with present-day North Carolina.[57] George Mason might have said with Horatio, "I am more an antique Roman than a Dane." By his involvement in the Ohio Company, he first glimpsed the transmontane civilization that Washington and the other Founding Fathers came to visualize for the United States, but his Antifederalist concept of government was smaller than theirs, too small to contain the vision. Bill of rights or no bill of rights, he could never reconcile himself to a national government in New York or Philadelphia. It was too big and too far away.[58] The parochial concerns from which others, including his Antifederalist allies, freed themselves remained with him to the end of his life. To high office he preferred the position of a country justice. This gave him enough scope for his adopted role as a tribune of the people. He needed a rostrum and contented himself, on occasion, with the one he found in the Fairfax County Court.

Footnotes

1. Mason to Thomas Jefferson, 27 Sept. 1781 (Robert A Rutland, ed., *The Papers of George Mason, 1725-1792* [3 vols.; Chapel Hill, 1970], II, 697) (hereafter cited as *Mason Papers*). Mason wrote to enlist Jefferson's opposition in the General Assembly to a move on foot in Congress to form new states form Virginia's territory west of the Alleghenies. Not only did he cite chapter and verse to show that this move violated specific provisions of the Articles of Confederation, but he denied the "industriously propagated" doctrine that the Revolution transferred sovereignty from Britain "'to the United States, that is to the American Congress.'" Thus early he stated the principles that sustained his Antifederalism.
2. Rowland, *The Life of George Mason, 1725-1792* (2 vols.; New York and London, 1892), I, 48-83.
3. Helen Hill, *George Mason: Constitutionalist* (Cambridge, Mass., 1938), pp. 15, 47-56, 268-70; Helen Hill Miller, *George Mason: Gentleman Revolutionary* (Chapel Hill, 1975), pp. 63, 77-79, 208; Pamela C. Copeland and Richard K. MacMaster, *The Five George Masons: Patriots and Planters of Virginia and Maryland* (Charlottesville, 1975), p. 168.
4. *Mason Papers*, I, cxiv.
5. Rutland, *George Mason: Reluctant Statesman* (Williamsburg, 1961), p. 24.
6. The surviving Fairfax County Court minutes (to 1792) on microfilm in the Virginia State Library are: Order Book, 1749 [16 May]-1754 [18 Jan.]; Order Book, 1754 [19 Jan.]-1756 [18 June]; Minute Book, 1756 [18 Aug.]-1763 [22 July]; Order Book, 1768 [15 Aug.]-1774 [22 Feb.]; Order Book, 1783 [16 June]-1792 [21 Feb.]. The gap 1763-68 is narrowed by a record book of the clerk's rough minutes, now in the Huntington Library, San Marino, Calif., and available on microfilm, starting on 16 Mar. 1763 and continuing through 17 Apr. 1765.

Subsequent references to Fairfax court proceedings recorded in the minutes are given by date only.
7. Beth Mitchell, *Beginning at a White Oak: Patents and Northern Neck Grants of Fairfax County, Virginia* (Fairfax, 1977), pp 326-27. Mason also inherited extensive properties in neighboring areas and in Charles County, Md.

8. H. R. McIlwaine et al., eds., *Executive Journals of the Council of Colonial Virginia* (6 vols.; Richmond, 1925-66), V, 231 (hereafter cited as *Exec. Journals*). Mason was sworn to his militia commission as colonel in Fairfax court on 22 July 1756, but he never commanded troops, his service being that of supply officer.
9. Charles S. Sydnor, *Gentlemen Freeholders: Political Practices in Washington's Virginia* (Chapel Hill, 1952), pp. 78-93 and passim.
10. *Ibid.*, pp. 78-93.
11. On court functions and ceremony, see A. G. Roeber, *Faithful Magistrates and Republican Lawyers: Creators of Virginia Legal Culture, 1680-1810* (Chapel Hill, 1981), pp. 73-95; Sydnor, *Gentlemen Freeholders*, pp. 84-90.
12. Copeland and MacMaster leave the opposite impression. They also accept too uncritically Mason's charge that the Alexandria merchants dominated the county court. In Mason's lifetime, planters held the judge's chair and enjoyed a majority in the quorum and the commission as a whole. Routinely, only four to eight justices sat, and one party might outvote the other by mustering more of its members (*The Five George Masons*, p. 168).
13. *Exec. Journals*, V, 379, 390.
14. Copeland and MacMaster, *The Five George Masons*, p. 152.
15. *Exec. Journals*, V, 276.
16. *Ibid.*, pp. 331-32.
17. *Ibid.*, pp. 378-79.
18. *Ibid.*, pp. 388-95. Roeber makes only passing mention of the purge (*Faithful Magistrates*, p. 114).
19. The reduced Fairfax commission consisted of: John Colvill, Lewis Ellzey, George William Fairfax, Stephen Lewis, Lawrence Washington, John West, John Carlyle, William Ramsay, Charles Broadwater, and Anthony Russell. Daniel McCarty was reappointed before the end of the year. Lawrence Washington died before the year was out; Stephen Lewis died in 1757. Colvill, Fairfax, or West held the judge's chair for the next twenty-five years (*Exec. Journals*, V, 390).
20. *Ibid.*, VI, 111.
21. It is assumed that the eighteen recommended by the Fairfax justices as a commission on 17 Nov. 1757 were subsequently named, and it appears they were.
The commission of 17 Feb. 1761 was recorded in Fairfax court on 17 Mar. 1761.
22. See Fairfax minutes, 21 Feb. 1759.
23. H. R. McIlwaine, ed., *Journals of the House of Burgesses of Virginia, 1758-1761* (Richmond, 1908), pp. 93, 99, 112, 119, 122, 123.
24. Mason to John Mercer, 11 Jan. 1764, quoted in Mercer to Charlton Palmer, 17 Apr. 1764; Mason to Edmund Randolph, 19 Oct. 1782 (*Mason Papers*, I, 58; II, 755).
25. H. R. McIlwaine, ed., "Justices of the Peace of Colonial Virginia, 1757-1775," *Bulletin of the Virginia State Library*, XIV (1921), 64. The commission is dated 7 Dec. 1764. December is apparently a mistake for November. No other commission appears in the Fairfax minutes between the one recorded, without date or list of names, on 21 Nov. 1764 and the date Mason qualified, 15 Apr. 1765. On a number of other occasions the list as printed is demonstrably erroneous. Of uncertain provenance, the list is possibly related to the "Commission book" referred to in 1784 (H. R. McIlwaine et al., eds., *Journals of the Council of the State of Virginia* [5 vols.; Richmond, 1931-82], III, 386) (hereafter cited as *JCS*).
26. See the commission of 13 June recorded in Fairfax court on 16 July 1770; *Exec. Journals*, VI, 348.
27. "A Plan of Government," [8-10 June 1776] (*Mason Papers*, I, 301); Madison to Jefferson, 16 Mar. 1784 (William T. Hutchinson et. al., eds., *The Papers of James*

Madison [Chicago and Charlottesville, 1962-   ], VIII, 9).
28. "Final Draft of the Virginia Constitution of 1776," [29 June 1776] (*Mason Papers*, I, 307).
29. "Fairfax County Petition Protesting Certain Actions by the Justices of the Peace," [8 June 1782] (*ibid.*, II, 733).
30. This episode is known only from Mason's highly colored 1782 account (*ibid.*, pp. 734-35). E. Lee Shepard treats this episode in the statewide context; Donald Sweig illuminates the wide range of issues for Fairfax County ("Courts in Conflict: Town-Country Relations in Post-Revolutionary Virginia," *Virginia Magazine of History and Biography*, LXXV [1977], 184-99; Nan Netherton, Donald Sweig, et al., *Fairfax County, Virginia: A History* [Fairfax, 1978], chap. V).
31. "Fairfax County Petition," [8 June 1782] (*Mason Papers*, II, 733-37); Roeber, *Faithful Magistrates*, p. 188.
32. This is easily the most disjointed political paper Mason ever circulated.
33. "Fairfax County Petition," 20 Nov. 1782 (*Mason Papers*, II, 737 n.); Roeber, *Faithful Magistrates*, p. 189.
34. "Deposition in a Lawsuit over Cargo of the Ship *General Washington*," [29 Sept. 1783] (*Mason Papers*, II, 789-90).
35. *JCS*, III, 385-86.
36. The seven signatories were Charles Broadwater, Alexander Henderson, Charles Alexander, David Stuart, George Gilpin, William Payne, and John Gibson. For some reason Mason did not sign, but his language is unmistakable. Other justices present who did not sign were David Arell, James Wren, and Edward Payne. The word "unanimously" was not corrected. Rutland prints the protest from a copy in the clerk's hand which lacks the signatories and contains minor variants from the text recorded in the minutes ("Protest from the Fairfax County Justices of the Peace," [22 Mar. 1785] [*Mason Papers*, II, 811-12]).
37. William Pierce, "Character Sketch of Delegates" (*ibid.*, III, 886-87 n.).
38. "Objections to this Constitution of Government," [ca. 16 Sept. 1787] (*ibid.*, 991-94 and n.). Washington to Madison, 10 Oct. 1787; Madison to Jefferson, 24 Oct. 1787 (Hutchinson et al., *Papers of Madison*, X, 189-90, 215).
39. "A Bill for Regulating the Rights of Cities, Towns and Boroughs, and the Jurisdiction of Corporation Courts," [24 Dec. 1787] (*Mason Papers*, III, 1025-26).
40. "Public Notice," 15 Nov. 1787 (*ibid.*, 1010, 1011 n.).
41. Madison to Jefferson, 24 Oct. 1787 (*ibid.*, p. 1007).
42. Madison to Washington, 23 June 1788; Edmund Randolph to Madison, 23 Oct. 1788 (Hutchinson et al., *Papers of Madison*, XI, 168, 314).
43. Mason to George Mason, Jr., 8 Jan. 1783 (*Mason Papers*, II, 761).
44. Rutland prints from a copy in the clerk's hand which contains minor variants. He does not refer to the remonstrance (*ibid.*, III, 1140-41).
45. *JCS*, V, 44, 48; William P. Palmer, ed., *Calendar of Virginia State Papers*, IV (Richmond, 1884), 553.
46. "Petition Seeking Removal of the Fairfax County Courthouse from Alexandria," attested 19 Oct. 1789 (*Mason Papers*, III, 1182-84 and n.).
47. *Ibid.*, p. 1184 n.
48. "Fairfax County Petition Protesting Delays in Selecting a Courthouse Site," [11 Nov. 1790] (*ibid.*, pp. 1211-15 and n.).
49. Mason to John Mason, 15 Mar. 1789 (*ibid.*, p. 1142).
50. This entire episode, including the letter, which is apparently printed here for the first time, has been overlooked by Mason scholars, but was cited by Donald Sweig (Netherton and Sweig, et al., *Fairfax County*, pp. 132-33).

51. Mason to Zachariah Johnston, 3 Nov. 1790 (*Mason Papers*, III, 1209).
52. Mason to Henry, 6 May 1783 (*ibid.*, II, 770).
53. Madison to Jefferson, 10 Dec. 1783 (*ibid.*, p. 791).
54. Julian P. Boyd, ed., *The Papers of Thomas Jefferson* (Princeton, 1950-), I, 606-7.
55. "Scheme for Replevying Goods and Distress for Rent," [23 Dec. 1765]; Mason to Monroe, 9 Feb. 1792 (*Mason Papers*, I, 62; III, 1258).
56. Boyd, *Papers of Jefferson*, II, 582 n.; but see Roeber for a review of post-Revolutionary change (*Faithful Magistrates*, pp. 171-202).
57. "Remarks on Annual Elections for the Fairfax Independent Company," [ca. 17-26 Apr. 1775] (*Mason Papers*, I, 231); Donald R. Dudley, *The Civilization of Rome* (New York, 1960), chap. III.
58. For this view, which prevailed among leading Antifederalists, see Cecilia M. Kenyon, "Men of Little Faith: The Anti-Federalists on the Nature of Representative Government," *William and Mary Quarterly*, 3d ser., XII (1955), 3-43; Stanley Elkins and Eric McKitrick, "The Founding Fathers: Young Men of the Revolution," *Political Science Quarterly*, LXXVI (1961), 181-216. Both are reprinted in Jack P. Greene, ed., *The Reinterpretation of the American Revolution, 1763-1789* (New York, 1968).

GEORGE MASON AND THE LEGACY OF CONSTITUTIONAL LIBERTY

An Examination of the Influence of George Mason on the American Bill of Rights

Section 2: The Constitution Years

"George Mason and the Constitution"
by Josephine F. Pacheco

"George Mason's 'Objections' and the Bill of Rights"
by Robert A. Rutland

"George Mason on the Tension Between Majority Rule and Minority Rights"
by Robert P. Davidow

GEORGE MASON AND THE CONSTITUTION

by Josephine F. Pacheco

When George Mason agreed to attend the Philadelphia Convention of 1787, he broke a lifelong rule against involvement in politics outside Virginia. His fellow Virginians, valuing his political wisdom, had consistently urged his participation in government, but he was always a reluctant office holder, even in Virginia. Although he was a member of the local county court and vestry, he attended their meetings only infrequently. Why then did Mason go to Philadelphia, spend the entire summer there, and assume an active role in the creation of the Constitution of 1787?

First of all, he did not want to see the Revolution destroyed. He had been one of the leaders in precipitating the War for Independence. Like many Americans in the 1780s, he feared that the United States might disintegrate; what he wanted was a strong, united country. How could he stand by and see his efforts come to nothing?

The second reason had to do with Mason's ownership of extensive agricultural property and the location of his home, Gunston Hall, on the Potomac River. The Potomac provided Gunston Hall with access, not only to the Maryland shore, but to the rest of the United States and to Europe. Mason, concerned about the establishment of effective trade patterns for his agricultural products, was alarmed at the difficult relations among the states and with foreign countries in the years after the Revolution. Hoping to reverse this pattern, he, along with Archibald Henderson, represented Virginia at the Mount Vernon Conference of 1785, which developed an effective agreement with Maryland on the use of the Potomac and other waterways. Although he did not attend the Annapolis Conference of the following year, he must have approved its call for a revision of the Articles of

Confederation, since he agreed to go to Philadelphia in 1787. Mason was looking beyond Virginia for ways to strengthen the new nation.

Although he was not a member of the bar, Mason's reputation for legal understanding was so great that he was deferred to in 1776 to be the major author of the Virginia Declaration of Rights and the state's first constitution. Since Virginia's leaders regarded him as a wise, trustworthy man, it is not surprising that they chose him as a member of the Virginia delegation to Philadelphia, though they must have been surprised when he accepted the appointment.

One hears constantly that James Madison had read widely in the history of the ancient republics. Although we know less about Mason's reading, he surely was familiar with the same sources as other learned Americans. He quoted Machiavelli, Montesquieu, and John Locke[1] and had thought deeply about the problems of representative government. He cited the experiences of the Greeks in defeating the Persians, the Dutch in holding off the Spanish, and the Swiss in maintaining independence "in the midst of the most powerful Nations."[2] The historian Forrest McDonald claims that Mason "had prestige not drastically beneath Washington's and talent that far outweighed Madison's."[3]

When Mason left Gunston Hall, he traveled by way of Annapolis and Baltimore, arriving in Philadelphia on May 17. Travel was very expensive — eight or nine dollars a day — but Philadelphia was cheap. He settled in at the Indian Queen Tavern on 4th Street, where he found satisfactory accommodations for 25s. Pennsylvania currency. That included servant and horses but not liquor.[4]

For a man who hated to be away from home as much as Mason did, it must have been exasperating to realize that the delegates were arriving one or two at a time: "the Members drop in slowly," he wrote. Since the Virginia delegation was complete — George Washington, James Madison, Edmund Randolph, George Wythe, James McClurg, and John Blair — the members began to meet every afternoon at the State House to hammer out a Virginia Plan for the Convention to consider. They conferred with delegates from the other states and with army officers in town for a meeting of the Society of the Cincinnati.[5]

Mason reported, even before the convention began, a surprising degree of unanimity on the form a new government should take. There would be, he said, "a total Alteration of the present foederal System and substituting a great National Council, or Parliament, consisting of two Branches of the Legislature, founded upon the Principles of equal proportionate Representation, with full legislative powers upon all the Objects of the Union . . . ." There would be an executive, an office that had not existed under the Articles of Confederation, though Mason did not yet have a clear notion of his powers. In spite of his awareness of the difficulty of organizing a government "upon this great Scale," and at the same time reserving sufficient power to the state legislatures "for promoting & securing the Prosperity & Happiness of their respective Citizens," Mason was optimistic. Success depended on "Coolness, Liberality & Candour," qualities he admitted were in short supply. He was proud that Virginia had taken the lead in proposing the outlines of a new government.[6]

Even before the Convention opened, Mason made clear his support for a strong, effective government and generally was in agreement with the ideas of Madison. It is an injustice to the memory of one of our truly great men to dismiss him by saying, "Oh, Mason didn't sign the Constitution." In fact, except for Madison, probably no one contributed more to the actual document than did Mason. He rightly deserves to be considered one of the fathers of our national government.

Mason was strongly committed to the success of the Convention. Soon after it opened, he wrote to his son that the eyes of Americans were focused on Philadelphia. "The revolt from Great Britain, & the Formations of our new Governments at that time, were nothing compared with the great Business now before us." Mason, from the beginning of the conflict, had been involved in resistance to Britain and in forming Virginia into a state: for him the creation of an effective central government was essential. He had thought seriously of "the Influence which the Establishments now proposed may have upon the Happiness or Misery of Millions yet unborn."[7] Mason believed that the existing government under the Articles was "approaching to Dissolution," that "without some material alterations it can not much longer subsist." The Convention had come into existence for "the protection[,] Safety & Happiness of the people."[8]

When it appeared that the Convention might collapse, Mason declared that though it was certainly inconvenient for him to remain in Philadelphia, he "would bury his bones in this City rather than expose his Country to the Consequences of a dissolution of the Convention without any thing being done." It could not be expected to create a perfect government, in spite of the "distinguished characters" participating, but Mason trusted to posterity for "the amendment of its defects, rather than to push the experiment too far." He cared so deeply about the success of the Philadelphia meeting that he acquiesced in the closed door policy adopted at the beginning. Only thus could the members avoid making "mistakes and misrepresentation until the business shall have been completed."[9] This seems strange doctrine from the man who defended freedom of speech and of the press, but the convention had to succeed.

Mason's remarks at the Convention make plain his determination to support a government with coercive powers. The new government should have the authority to suppress rebellions against particular states. Otherwise, "As Rebellions agst. [sic] itself [the federal government] originate in and agst. [sic] individual States, it must not remain a passive Spectator of its own subversion."[10]

The new government should have the power to regulate the militia. Since he hoped that there would be no standing army in time of peace, "unless it might be for a few garrisons," the militia ought to be prepared to defend the country. The thirteen states could never agree on any one system; "if they [the states] will not give up the power over the whole, they probably will over a part as a select militia."[11]

In 1788 the Antifederalists, of whom Mason would be a leader, would object most strenuously to congressional control over the militia. Nevertheless, Mason's support of such power in the summer of 1787 demonstrates his conviction that the central government had to have real authority.

Not once but twice during the Convention Mason urged that Congress be given the power to enact sumptuary laws: "No Government can be maintained unless the manners be made consonant to it." After speaking of "the extravagance of our manners, the excessive consumption of foreign superfluities, and the necessity of restricting it," he asked for a committee "to report articles of association for encouraging by the advice the influence and the example of the members of the Convention, oeconomy frugality and American manufactures." Mason got such a committee, but it never reported.[12] Surely there is no greater power that a government can have than the right to regulate personal behavior.

Mason participated significantly in discussions on the structure of the government. Since he plainly favored a tripartite division of power, it is therefore convenient to consider his thoughts on the three branches, executive, judicial, legislative. When it came to the creation of an executive — and he was sure that there should be an executive separate from the legislature — he hoped to see a strong executive made up of three men representing the three major areas of the country: northern, middle, and southern. By this device the government could receive exact information on sectional interests. The three men could be the means of "checking and counteracting the aspiring Views of dangerous and ambitious Men," and would make sure the government was based on "the invaluable Principles of Liberty." Nevertheless, when the convention agreed on a single executive, Mason went along, though he insisted on such an official having a single seven year term with no possibility of reelection.[13]

He did not support the proposal that the executive should serve "during good behavior." In the first place, it would be impossible to define misbehavior in such a way as to bring the executive to trial, nor would it be possible to compel such a person to submit to trial. "He considered an Executive during good behavior as a softer name only for an Executive for life." The next step would be hereditary monarchy, perhaps in his lifetime, but certainly in that of his children or grandchildren.[14]

Impeachment was his preferred device for removing the chief ex-executive. "Shall any man be above Justice? Above all shall that man be above it, who can commit the most extensive injustice? When great crimes were committed he was for punishing the principal as well as the Coadjutors." There spoke the student of 17th century English history, for just so had Justice Edward Coke spoken to the king: No man can be above the law. On the other hand, Mason did not want to make it easy for the legislature to remove the executive, for to make him the "mere creature of the Legislature" was to violate "the fundamental principle of good Government." The executive should have only a suspensive veto, with the legislature having the right to pass a law over his veto with a larger majority.[15]

The method of choosing an executive caused great difficulty for all the members of the convention. Mason rejected popular election for two reasons: 1) the Society of the Cincinnati would control the election and 2) the large extent of the country made it impossible for the people to have "the requisite capacity to judge of the respective pretensions of the Candidates." He therefore decided that election by the legislature would be the best method, though he worried about intrigues between the executive and the legislature.[16]

In the course of the discussions over the executive, Mason stated his political philosophy in the clearest terms: "Having for his primary object, for the pole-star of his political conduct, the preservation of the rights of the people, he held it as an essential point, as the very palladium of Civil liberty, that the great officers of State, and particularly the Executive should at fixed periods return to that mass from which they were at first taken, in order that they may feel and respect those rights & interests, which are again to be personally valuable to them."[17] Mason had held such a belief in 1776 when he wrote the Virginia Declaration of Rights and the Virginia Constitution; eleven years later he had not changed his mind.

Mason and Madison wrote a major portion of the oath that the president takes when he is sworn into office.

Mason contributed little to debates over the judiciary, though he favored a federal judiciary, which did not exist under the Articles of Confederation. He wanted legislative appointment of the members of the court, but he recognized the right of the court "to declare an unconstitutional law void."[18] Although the Constitution as finally adopted did not specifically give the Federal judiciary such authority, Mason took for granted the check on the power of the legislature. On the other hand, he seems to have been concerned that the federal judiciary would "swallow up" the state courts.[19]

In the definition of treason, one of the very important passages of the Constitution, Mason contributed the words "giving them [the enemy] aid and comfort."[20]

Mason was deeply concerned about the legislature. He spent more time on the House of Representatives than on any other part of the new government. This was because he envisioned it as the branch of government closest to the people and most responsive to their will. Nothing was more important than popular election of members of the lower house: "Whatever inconveniency may attend the democratic principle," he said, it was "the only security for the rights of the people."[21]

Elections should be held every two years instead of annually so that the representatives of distant states could arrive on time for congressional sessions. It was Mason who insisted that members of the House had to be at least 25 years old. "It had been said that Congs [sic] had proved a good school for our young men. It might be so for any thing he knew but if it were, he chose that they should bear the expence [sic] of their own education." When it came to the question of how to apportion representatives, Mason opposed counting wealth of any kind, including slaves. Only population should be considered in fixing a state's representation in the national legislature.[22] To count wealth would probably increase Virginia's representation, but Mason opposed it for reasons of fairness.

Mason's vision of what the House of Representatives should be is shown in a number of points that he emphasized:

1) Periodic reapportionment was essential. As the South and West grew, their population would outstrip that of the existing states. If something were not done to force redistricting, the government would soon be in the hands of a minority. "From the nature of man we may be sure, that those who have power in their hands will not give it up while they can retain it. On the contrary we know they will always when they can rather increase it."[23] That, of course is the reason for the decennial census: to be sure that the House of Representatives follows the population. In view of the outrage expressed whenever a state loses representation as a result of the census, one must admit that Mason was very wise in assessing a state's reluctance to lose power.

2) Representatives had to live in the districts they represented in order to acquire "local knowledge." Otherwise, said he, "Rich men of neighboring States, may employ with success the means of corruption in some particular district and thereby get into the public Councils after having failed in their own State." This was the practice in England, and he thought it a very bad one.[24]

3) A person had to have been a citizen for seven years before becoming eligible for election to the lower house.[25]

4) Nothing was as important as limiting money bills to the House of Representatives. He returned to that over and over, during the entire summer. Mason understood, perhaps better than any other member of the Convention, that where the money was, there was the power. Since the House of Representatives was the only body directly responsive to the will of the people, it alone should have the authority to determine how the people's money would be spent. If the

Senate had the power of giving away the people's money, "they might soon forget the source from when[ce] they received it. We might soon have an aristocracy."[26]

Although Mason was an ardent supporter of popular election for the members of the lower house, he was equally determined that the state legislatures should choose the members of the upper house, seeing this as essential for the preservation of state governments. The Senate would be the means "to secure the rights of property," and he thought a property qualification for senators a good idea. A six year term for senators would "give them weight and firmness." Two senators per state would be the best number, and they should have lived in the United States for 14 years (the number finally agreed on was nine).[27]

Mason came to distrust the Senate, speaking of its "aristocratic influence." He wanted it to have no part in selection of the president: If electors did not choose the executive, then the House of Representatives should. He opposed the office of vice president, regarding that office as "an encroachment on the rights of the Senate."[28] Mason plainly believed in the complete separation of powers.

Mason was not successful in all his proposals. The original Virginia plan, presented by Edmund Randolph at the beginning of the Convention, had included a proposal for a Council of Revision that would have "a Negative upon our Laws." When others gave up such an idea, Mason clung to it, feeling that such a council would serve as a "restraining power" on the legislature, which might be expected to pass "unjust and pernicious laws." If such a council existed, it would discourage "demagogues" from trying to secure the passage of bad laws. Early in the Convention, Mason proposed a council that would include both the executive and the judiciary. By the end of the summer of 1787, he was supporting a council of six members, chosen by the Senate, that would represent the three sections of the country, eastern, central, and southern. Without such a council, the United States was "about to try an experiment on which the most despotic Governments had never ventured." Nevertheless, his arguments failed to convince the Convention.[29]

The members of the Convention could not avoid the issue of slavery, and though they refused to face the basic one of its abolition, they dealt with several other aspects of the problem. First, should slaves count as people or property when apportioning representation in the House of Representatives? Mason admitted that bondsmen raised the value of land, could provide food and support for an army in time of war, and in times of emergency might become soldiers. For those reasons they ought to have some share in counting the population — not in voting —, but Mason "could not . . . regard them as equal to freemen and could not vote for them as such."[30]

Two additional questions concerning slaves were their continuing importation into the United States and their being taxed on entering the country. Mason opposed allowing additional slaves to enter the country, but if they were brought in, they should be taxed. The decision of the Convention was to allow — or, more precisely, not to forbid — the importation of slaves for twenty years, with a maximum duty of ten dollars per head. The Virginia delegation voted against that provision.

Mason spoke eloquently about the evils of slavery:

> Slavery discourages arts & manufactures. The poor despise labor when performed by slaves. They prevent the immigration of Whites, who really enrich & strengthen a Country. They produce the most pernicious effect on manners. Every master of slaves is born a petty tyrant. They bring the judgment of heaven on a Country. As nations can not be rewarded or punished in the next world they must be in this. By an inevitable chain of causes & effects providence punishes national sins, by national calamities.

But what Mason asked for was not an end to slavery but "that the Genl. Govt. should have power to prevent the increase of slavery."[31]

In addition to the structure of the Constitution, Mason made many other contributions. He proposed that the seat of government should be fixed at some place other than a state capital. One could argue that Mason was thus responsible for the District of Columbia. He favored publishing the proceedings of Congress. Congress rather than the executive should have the power to declare war. Congress should meet annually "as essential to the preservation of the Constitution." He did not doubt that the country would supply enough business, though the fact that anybody would have doubts along that line demonstrates how small the country was in 1787.[32]

Nothing was of more concern to Mason than the questions of trade and the taxation of exports. Since the South, the region that Mason called "the staple states," exported agricultural products, it would be particularly vulnerable to taxation. Therefore, he urged that Congress should be forbidden to impose export taxes, and this became part of the Constitution. If the North took advantage of the South by taxing agricultural exports, it would be an example of the majority oppressing the minority. "If the Govt. [sic] is to be lasting, it must be founded in the confidence & affections of the people, and must be so constructed as to obtain these."[33]

Whatever Mason said at the Convention was colored by the fact that he was a firm believer in republican government and was sure that the American people felt the same way. He feared the corruption of luxury and never relaxed his vigilance to prevent a small group, a "Junto," from ruling the country. Furthermore, he favored admitting western states on a basis of equality with the original ones. People would surely go west, "and the best policy is to treat them with that equality which will make them friends not enemies." He sought to protect the right of free white males to vote and thought that heads of families, even if they were not property holders, had an interest in good government and should vote. Toward the end of his life, Mason described himself as a stern republican, and his actions during the convention confirm this.[34]

In spite of all his constructive work on the new Constitution, in the end Mason refused to sign. In the last weeks of the Convention he joined with Edmund Randolph in proposing many changes that he believed essential for the working of the government. Finally he decided that a new convention was necessary and listed the reasons that he would not put his name to the Constitution.

At the head of his list, and in the long run the most important item, he wrote, "There is no Declaration of Rights." When he raised this point at the Convention, people pointed out that there were state bills of rights that would provide adequate protection for the individual. Not so, said Mason, for the laws passed under the new Constitution would be "paramount to the laws and constitution of the several States." Therefore, without specific written protections, the people might lose their rights.[35] Of all that happened in 1787, nothing was more important than this, for it was Mason's insistence that led to the eventual adoption of the first ten amendments to the Constitution.

Mason concluded that the new government had too many powers, and none so alarmed him (beyond the absence of a bill of rights) as the danger that the northern states would pass commercial laws that would destroy the South. All laws regulating trade should require a two-thirds majority to become law.[36] Here Mason was anticipating the alarm of the South, so often stated by John C. Calhoun in the 19th century, that the government encouraged the tyranny of the majority.

Mason's refusal to sign the Constitution and his firm opposition to Virginia's ratification earned him the anger of James Madison and the confirmed dislike of George Washington. He and Madison were later reconciled, but the friendship of Washington was gone forever. Mason particularly lamented this, for they had been friends since their youth, but he wrote, "I am truly conscious of having acted from the purest motives of honesty, and love to my country, according to that measure of judgment which God has bestowed on me, and I would not forfeit the approbation of my own mind for the approbation of any man, or all the men upon earth."[37]

As one studies the proceedings of the Convention of 1787, Mason's statesmanship becomes evident. All during that hot summer he spoke out for effective government that would protect the rights of the people. He feared monarchy and aristocracy, but he never doubted the need for government that could hold the country together and encourage growth. In this bicentennial year Mason does not receive his fair share of attention. Madison gets credit for the bill of rights, whereas he opposed the concept and agreed to support such a document only as a last resort. Mason is brushed aside as an opponent of the Constitution, whereas the truth is that he was a major contributor to its creation. As a part of our bicentennial celebration, it is essential to remember his firm adherence to the principles of republicanism, and his determination, in spite of all obstacles, to see that the rights of the individual were never abridged.

Footnotes

1. *The Papers of George Mason, 1725-1792*, ed. Robert A. Rutland, 3 vols. (Chapel Hill: University of North Carolina Press, 1970) 3:1050.
2. *Ibid.*, 3:897.
3. Forrest McDonald, *E Pluribus Unum: The Formation of the American Republic, 1776-1790*, 2d ed. (Indianapolis: Liberty Press, 1979), p. 265.
4. Mason to Edmund Randolph, April 23, 1787; id. to George Mason, Jr., May 20, 1787, *Mason Papers*, 3:876, 879, 881.
5. Mason to George Mason, Jr., May 20, 1787, ibid., 3:879-80.
6. *Id.* to *id.*, May 20, June 1, 1787, *ibid.*, 3:880, 892.
7. *Id.* to *id.*, June 1, 1787, *ibid.*, 3:892-93.
8. *Mason Papers*, 3:903-4; Max Farrand, ed., *The Records of the Federal Convention of 1787*, 4 vols. (New Haven: Yale University Press, 1937), 4:75-76. Rutland thinks Mason may not have written these words, but he wrote about the same thing to Arthur Lee on May 21. *Mason Papers*, 3:882.
9. *Mason Papers*, 3:920; *Notes of Debates in the Federal Convention of 1787 Reported by James Madison*, ed. Adrienne Koch (Athens, Ohio: Ohio University Press, 1966), pp. 243-44; *Mason Papers*, 3:908; *Madison*, pp. 157-59; Mason to George Mason, Jr., May 27, 1787, *Mason Papers*, 3:884.
10. *Mason Papers*, 3:927; *Madison*, p.321.
11. *Mason Papers*, 3:960-61; *Madison*, p. 478.
12. *Mason Papers*, 3:962, 982; *Madison*, pp. 488, 632.

13. *Mason Papers*, 3:897-88, 894; *Madison*, p. 49.
14. *Mason Papers*, 3:926; *Madison*, p. 312.
15. *Mason Papers*, 3:927, 895, 899: *Madison*, pp. 331-32, 56, 64-5.
16. *Mason Papers*, 3:931-32, 925, 894: *Madison*, pp. 370-71, 308-9, 49.
17. *Mason Papers*, 3:931-32; *Madison*, pp. 370-71.
18. *Mason Papers*, 3:928-29; *Madison*, pp. 341-42, 346.
19. Although the memorandum containing this view was in the handwriting of Pierce Butler, James Hutson believes that he copied it from one written by Mason. James H. Hutson, ed. *Supplement to Max Farrand's The Records of the Federal Convention of 1787.* (New Haven; Yale University Press, 1987), p. 249n.
20. *Mason Papers*, 3:963; *Madison*, p. 493.
21. *Mason Papers*, 3:910; *Madison*, p. 167.
22. *Mason Papers*, 3:911, 912, 924-25; *Madison*, pp. 170, 174, 270, 284.
23. *Mason Papers*, 3:924, 922; *Madison*, pp. 273-74, 266.
24. *Mason Papers*, 3:950-51; *Madison*, p. 408.
25. *Mason Papers*, 3:950; *Madison*, p. 406
26. *Mason Papers*, 3:952, 955-57, 964, 919-20, 921; *Madison*, pp. 417, 442-44, 496, 250.
27. *Mason Papers*, 3:915, 930, 953; *Madison*, pp. 190-91, 200, 354, 419.
28. *Mason Papers*, 3:975-79: *Madison*, pp. 577, 583-86, 592, 596-97.
29. *Mason Papers*, 3:928, 901, 979: *Madison*, pp. 341-42, 81, 600-01.
30. *Mason Papers*, 3:323; *Madison*, pp. 268-69.
31. *Mason Papers*, 3:968-69, 965-66: *Madison*, pp. 532, 503-04.
32. *Mason Papers*, 3:933, 960, 948-49; *Madison*, pp. 378, 476, 399.
33. *Mason Papers*, 3:958-59, 964-65, 972-73: *Madison*, pp. 466-67, 501, 549-50.
34. *Mason Papers*, 3:907, 913, 973, 949-50: *Madison*, pp. 158, 177, 552, 403: Mason to Thomas Marshall, Oct. 16, 1789, *Mason Papers*, 3:1175.
35. Objections to this Constitution of Government," [ca. Sept, 16, 1787], *Mason Papers*, 3:991.
36. *Ibid.*, 3:992.
37. Mason to John Mason, March 13, 1789, *ibid.*, 3:1142.

GEORGE MASON'S "OBJECTIONS" AND THE BILL OF RIGHTS

by Robert Rutland

In 1787 George Mason was a political figure to be reckoned with, spoken of in the same breath with Virginians Washington, Jefferson, Madison, Patrick Henry, and Richard Henry Lee. He was, as they said then, "a man of parts"; Jefferson described him as "of the first order of greatness." The chief author of the Virginia Declaration of Rights in 1776, Mason had been either a legislator or a confidant in the Revolutionary councils of the Old Dominion from 1774 onward. Now, from May to September in 1787, Mason was a key member of his state's delegation at the Federal Convention, a frequent and persuasive speaker, and the man who played a vital role in such matters as presidential impeachment and fiscal responsibility.

But Mason did not approve of the outcome of the Constitutional Convention. He made significant last-minute motions on the Convention floor, and one which his colleagues rejected returned to haunt them: Mason belatedly called for the addition of a bill of rights to the Constitution. Mason's call was shaped into a motion by Elbridge Gerry. They must have witnessed the roll call of states with chagrin as the resolution "to prepare a Bill of Rights" was defeated unanimously.

Then and later the Federalists were short-tempered when the subject of a bill of rights arose. Delegate Roger Sherman was their spokesman when he helped derail Mason's motion. Stating that he too was "for securing the rights of the people where requisite," Sherman continued, that "the State Declarations of Rights are not repealed by this Constitution; and being in force are sufficient." Moreover, Sherman contended, "the Legislature may be safely trusted." James

Madison sided with Sherman and five days later, thirty-nine of Mason's colleagues (one by proxy) signed the Constitution. Mason, Gerry, and Edmund Randolph (who also declined to sign), watched the convention approve the Constitution, according to Dr. Franklin's motion, "by the unanimous consent of *the States* present."

Franklin's tactic placed the trio of naysayers on the defensive, an awkward position for one like Mason who had been so hopeful at the start of the enterprise. Mason had come to Philadelphia that spring convinced that "the Eyes of the United States are turn'd upon this Assembly, & their Expectations raised to a very anxious Degree." "May God grant we may be able to gratify them," Mason prayed in June 1787. Along with James Wilson and James Madison, Mason had engaged articulately in debates on behalf of enlarging participation. Mason's arguments for popular election of the lower house in Congress, his insistence on the right to impeach a corrupt president, and his approval of presidential elections by a direct vote of the citizenry all fitted his philosophical commitment to a broad-based republic. A slaveowner and man of means, Mason had also denounced the slave trade.

At the same time, Mason sought to keep the Union from swallowing the states, and thus he supported selection of senators by the state legislatures and vowed "he never would agree to abolish the State govts. or render them absolutely insignificant." Mason also adamantly sought protection for southern shipping interests in the form of a two-thirds majority for commercial legislation. Within his own guidelines, Mason steadily argued for a government that trusted the people over the privileged. Fellow delegate William Pierce said of Mason: "He is able and convincing in debate, steady and firm in his principles, and undoubtedly one of the best politicians in America."

After nearly four months of give and take, compromise and bullying, the delegates had survived and so had their Constitution; but in Mason's view the convention still gave too little attention given to citizens' rights. Mason distrusted

"OBJECTIONS" AND THE BILL OF RIGHTS

the final draft as a protector of individual citizen or of the southern planting economy. During that last week, Mason recorded his misgivings about the Constitution on the back of the printed report of the Committee of Style, beginning simply: "There is no Declaration of Rights." From that preamble, Mason proceeded to list what he called his "Objections to this Constitution of Government."

His original list of objections claimed that the Constitution upset the English common law, made Congress into a kind of oligarchy, allowed the federal courts to destroy state ones, and left the presidency rudderless without a "Constitutional Council." Mason feared that without the latter, a natural cabinet "will grow out of the principal officers of the great departments; the worst and most dangerous of all ingredients for such a Council in a free country." The created office of the Vice President, Mason thought, was disastrous and unnecessary, since the incumbent "for want of other employment is made president of the Senate, thereby dangerously blending the executive and legislative powers."

As for the presidential powers, Mason thought the chief executive might misuse his "unrestrained power of granting pardons for treason" and might "screen from punishment those whom he had secretly instigated to commit the crime, and thereby prevent a discovery of his own guilt." The president's treaty-making powers, combined with senatorial approval, made such pacts the supreme law of the land without any scrutiny by the people's branch of government — the House of Representatives. And by allowing a congressional majority to pass laws restricting American commerce "the five Southern States, whose product and circumstances are totally different from that of the eight Northern and Eastern States, may be ruined."

Mason also lambasted the vague construction of the Constitution and foresaw the "general welfare" clause as a catchall term bound to be abused. Although Mason specifically called for declarations of freedom of the press and trial by jury, he lamented the ban on *ex post facto* laws in the state legislatures since "there never was nor can be a legislature but must and will make such laws, when necessity and the public safety require them."

Gloomy to the end, Mason predicted that without an immediate ban on slave trading the nation would be "weaker, more vulnerable, and less capable of defense," and under the Constitution would "set out [as] a moderate aristocracy" then degenerate into either a monarchy or "tyrannical aristocracy." "It will," he predicted, "most probably vibrate some years between the two, and then terminate in the one or the other."

First as a handwritten text and then as a printed pamphlet, Mason's "Objections" made the rounds in Philadelphia's political circles during the last two weeks of September. From the opening phrase of his "Objections" to the bill of rights that James Madison offered in Congress two years later, the line is so direct that we can say Mason forced Madison's hand. Federalist supporters of the Constitution could never overcome the protest created by Mason's phrase: "There is no Declaration of Rights." Months later, Hamilton was still trying "to kill that snake" in *Federalist* No. 84. Oliver Ellsworth's "Landholder" essays in 1787-88, perhaps more influential at the time than the papers of "Publius," also made a frontal attack on Mason's "Objections," as did Federalist James Iredell in North Carolina in 1788.

But the idea was too powerful. Mason's pamphlet soon circulated along the Atlantic seaboard and by the onset of winter the "Objections" had appeared in newspapers in Virginia and New Jersey. Mason himself paid for a second printing and sent Washington the pamphlet early in October, claiming that "a little Moderation & Temper, in the latter End of the Convention, might have removed" his misgivings.

Mason also mailed one to Jefferson, then at his diplomatic post in Paris, explaining that "These Objections of mine were first printed very incorrectly, without my Approbation, or Privity; which laid me under some kind of Necessity of publishing them afterwards, myself....You will find them conceived in general Terms; as I wished to confine them to a narrow Compass." Mason went on to add to his list

"OBJECTIONS" AND THE BILL OF RIGHTS 79

objections related to regulating the state militia, to the potential power to abuse the election process, and the power of congressmen to raise their own salaries. "But it wou'd be tedious to enumerate all the Objections," Mason concluded, "and I am sure they cannot escape Mr. Jefferson's Observation."

But whatever his other objections, it was the issue of the bill of rights that struck Jefferson. Not long after Mason's pamphlet reached Jefferson's desk in Paris the American minister was writing to friends at home in outspoken terms. Jefferson told Madison he liked the Constitution but was alarmed by "the omission of a bill of rights," and, to John Adams's son-in-law, Jefferson said bluntly: "Were I in America, I would advocate it [the Constitution] warmly till nine states should have adopted, and then as warmly take the other side to convince the remaining four that they ought not to come into it till the declaration of rights is annexed to it."

In a backhanded way, Jefferson's plan became the model. Alarmed by Anti-Federalist strategy that aimed at a second federal convention, friends of the Constitution wanted to derail any scheme for another national gathering. Although Madison was concerned that a bill of rights would offer little real protection and by enumerating some rights put others in jeopardy, if concessions on the bill-of-rights issue could forestall demands for a second convention, Federalists came to realize they must pay that price. Starting at the Massachusetts ratifying convention in February 1788, Federalists in charge of counting votes abandoned their adamant position and began to talk about "recommendatory amendments."

By conceding that a bill of rights ought to be considered by the first Congress, Madison and his co-workers whittled away at the Anti-Federalist majority in Virginia. Their concession on a bill of rights made it easier for committed Anti-Federalist delegates to swallow the bitter pill of ratification, and in Virginia the Federalists' gesture also gave proponents of the Constitution a way to defend a vote in opposition to Patrick Henry and Mason, who were still not assuaged. As they saw their majority melting away, Henry and Mason wanted their proposed amendments, including a bill of rights, to be a condition for Virginia's ratification. When the convention rejected that tactic and voted instead, as the Massachusetts delegates had done, for "recommendatory" amendments, the game for the staunchest Anti-Federalists was over. The Constitution was quickly ratified.

But James Madison had learned his lesson. A few months later, when he ran for a seat in that first Congress, Madison had to assure constituents that "it is my sincere opinion that the Constitution ought to be revised." What changes would he seek? Nothing less than a bill of rights containing "the most satisfactory provisions for all essential rights, particularly the rights of Conscience in the fullest latitude, the freedom of the press, trials by jury, security against general warrants &c." It seems unlikely that Madison would have made such an about-face without the storm of protest first raised by Mason's "Objections."

By not signing the Constitution, Mason had gained a principle but lost a friend. Or almost so, for a painful estrangement between Madison and himself did not abate until Madison introduced a bill of rights in Congress in September 1789. Mason quickly praised the provisions in a letter to Congressman Samuel Griffin from Virginia, knowing his letter would be seen Madison. "I have received much Satisfaction from the Amendments to the federal Constitution, which have lately passed the House of Representatives," Mason wrote, "I hope they will also pass the Senate. With two or three further Amendments ... I cou'd chearfully put my Hand & Heart to the new Government."

One of the most self-effacing men ever to serve the American people, Mason regretted the tensions that grew out of the ratification struggle. Eventually, he welcomed Madison and Jefferson back to his home at Gunston Hall, and their friendship fell into the old grooves. But Mason's standing as a "founding father" was long under a cloud, owing chiefly to his stance on the Constitution. His patriotic service in preparing the Fairfax Resolves in 1774, his cardinal role at the Virginia Convention of 1776, his authorship of that state bill of rights, his authorship of both the Virginia bill of rights and constitution (the latter endured until 1829), and his offering of time, talent, and money to the American cause between 1776 and 1781 became only dim memories, hardly mentioned in the standard histories. By the early twentieth century, however, attention to civil liberties began to increase and scholars came to note the original role Mason played when he insisted on constitutional protection for a free press and other civil rights. By 1988, Mason was beginning to reap some of the acclaim he deserved for his simple warning: "There is no Declaration of Rights."

GEORGE MASON ON THE TENSION BETWEEN MAJORITY RULE AND MINORITY RIGHTS[*]

by Robert Davidow[**]

Biographical Note[1]

If this were an article about the views of Washington, Jefferson, or Madison, it would hardly be necessary to provide biographical information. Because George Mason is still relatively unknown, however, it is appropriate to begin with a biographical sketch to provide a context in which to evaluate his views.

Born in 1725 in very comfortable circumstances in Dogue's Neck, Virginia (a peninsula bounded on three sides by Pohick Creek, the Potomac River, and Occoquan Creek), Mason was brought up principally by his mother and an uncle, John Mercer, following the death of his father in 1735. His education apparently consisted of attendance at a small school, private tutoring at home, and reading in John Mercer's private library, a most considerable library for the day that included many law books.

A good deal of Mason's life was devoted to his family (a wife and nine children) and to the management of his plantation at Gunston Hall, which was completed in 1758. The plantation was quite self-sufficient; the work was performed by over 100 slaves. Mason also devoted considerable energy to the work of the Ohio Company, of which he was the treasurer for many years. (The Ohio Company claimed and planned to develop western lands.)

Like his friend and neighbor George Washington, Mason was active in local affairs. He was, for example, a justice of the peace,[2] a vestryman of Truro Parish (Anglican), and trustee of the Town of Alexandria. He also became involved in colonial affairs, for example as a delegate to the House of Burgesses from 1758 to 1761.

MAJORITY RULE AND MINORITY RIGHTS

Beginning in 1765, with the parliamentary passage of the hated Stamp Act, Mason increasingly involved himself in colonial activities that led to the break with the British Crown. In 1776 he wrote the first draft of the Virginia Declaration of Rights and participated in the work resulting in the final declaration; he also participated in the drafting or the State Constitution of that year. He served in the Virginia House of Delegates from 1776 to 1780. In 1784 and 1785 he served on the Virginia-Maryland commission dealing with questions pertaining to the Potomac River. Also, in 1785 he assisted Madison in the effort to block subsides for "teachers of the Christian Religion."

In 1786 Mason was appointed as part of the delegation to the constitutional convention scheduled for 1787 in Philadelphia. He was a very active and constructive participant in that convention until almost the very end, when his attitude changed and he voiced opposition to the Constitution, which he refused to sign. The following year, 1788, he was elected as delegate to the state ratifying convention and opposed the ratification of the Constitution in that convention. In 1790 he was appointed to a vacant United States Senate seat, but refused to serve. He died in 1792 at Gunston Hall.

The Issue

Of the many views expressed by Mason during his lifetime, those that bear on the tension between majority rule and minority rights are of special interest today in light of the continuing debate on that subject, in which representatives of the Reagan administration have been very prominent. A study of Mason's views on this subject not only can satisfy our curiosity about an intrinsically interesting period of American history, but also can illumine the "original" understanding of this issue and the difficulties associated with the attempt to apply this original understanding to contemporary events.

The question is, on the assumption that some form of democracy is to function in a particular society, are there nevertheless some limitations, beyond those encountered in getting a law enacted in the first instance, on the power of a majority to impose its will on the minority or the individual?[3]

The relatively recent history in the United States has shown that, although the issue is still a lively one, persons on both sides of the issue, or their ideological descendants, have changed places. In the early part of the twentieth century, and indeed until the mid-1930s, many of those emphasizing majority rule sought a more forceful role for the federal and state legislatures in economic regulation;[4] conversely, those resisting majority rule were, or tended to be, concerned mainly with the protection of rights of property.[5] In the last thirty years or so, many of those who were previously champions of majority rule have become champions of a more limited form of democracy,[6] whereas at least some of those who formerly favored restraints upon the legislature now argue for legislative action unrestrained by judicial review.[7]

Before we proceed to a consideration of Mason's views — a consideration that will focus on Mason's role in helping to draft the Virginia Declaration of Rights in 1776,[8] his participation in the debates of the Federal Constitutional Convention of 1787,[9] and his role at the ratifying convention in Virginia in 1788 (at which, as a non-signer of the Constitution, he opposed its ratification without prior amendments)[10] — it is necessary to define, at least for purposes of this article, the terms "majority rule" and "minority rights." First, it is necessary to note that the basic issue here — the tension between permitting the majority to have its way and simultaneously protecting minorities in certain ways — is independent of any substantive issue. That is, as illustrated by the changing composition of those supporting and opposing unlimited majority rule, supporters of any substantive political position can be either in favor of or against restraint on the ability of the majority to enact its views into law. Nevertheless, it is always possible that one's views about particular substantive issues will color one's attitude towards this particular tension.[11] For example, since the current attorney general of the United States, Edwin Meese III, has argued for greater majority rule (and thus less judicial review by the Supreme Court),[12] one who is politically opposed to some of the substantive positions that Meese has espoused may be tempted to argue in favor of a greater role for judicial review in order to effect political results more in accordance with one's own political views. I hope that, being aware of the problem, I will be less inclined than I might otherwise be to engage in "selective perception"[13] both in the definition of the issue and in the selection of pertinent historical materials. I have to concede, however, that, being human, I am not likely to succeed completely.

It is not enough merely to say that the terms "majority rule" and "minority rights" are unrelated to substantive legal issues; one must go beyond this and decide whether a particular attitude is indeed characteristic of a championing of majority rule over minority rights. The determination of this issue is not always easy. First, one must decide what constitutes majority rule. Is it rule by the original super-majority that ratified the Constitution and the Bill of Rights?[14] Or is it rule by a simple majority of citizens considering a question today? The latter is the sense in which I shall use the term "majority rule." (Use of the concept of the original ratifying super-majority would cause semantic confusion and obscure the real tension between what a current majority may wish to do and the interests of a current minority.)[15]

Another complication is illustrated by the notion of representative, as contrasted with direct, democracy. Some delegates suggested during the debates in Philadelphia in 1787 that the majority was to be feared;[16] others said that the real problem was the danger of arbitrary action by governmental officials (apparently in disregard of the wishes of the majority).[17] Arguably, only the former position is illustrative of a desire to protect minority rights; the latter position is seemingly consistent with a desire to maintain majority rule by simply forcing the government (consisting of representatives of the people) to carry out the will of the majority. As a practical matter, it may be difficult to maintain this distinction because, unless a government utilizes a public opinion poll to determine the attitudes of the public on a regular basis, it will sometimes not be clear — how often it is difficult to say — that a particular government or governmental official is acting contrary to the wishes of the majority of the people. Moreover, structures intended to prevent a minority faction from implementing its will can make it more difficult for a true majority of the population to have its will reflected in legislation. In other words, various forms of checks and balances (for example, the division of the legislature into two houses differently constituted) can frustrate the popular will as well as the will of factions. In any event, a principal characteristic of a representative democracy is that the populace does not vote continually on specific issues but rather chooses individuals who are to represent the populace in making basic policy decisions.[18] Thus it may be appropriate, as a practical matter, to consider statements in favor of limits on governmental action as consistent with the protection of the minority even if there is an expression of concern that governmental officials may act arbitrarily and in disregard of the majority's view. Certainly, judicial review, in the sense of judicial declaration of the invalidity of *legislative action*, would seem to involve the notion of the protection of the minority against majority rule inasmuch as the legislature must be presumed to act generally in accordance with the wishes of a majority of the population; the probability that representatives who regularly ignore the wishes of their constituents will be defeated at the next election supports this presumption. (The same presumption ought to apply to acts of the President, since the President is elected as the representative of the whole people.)[19]

What follows is first an investigation of Mason's views showing hostility to unfettered majority rule in certain areas — for example, natural law/natural rights, bills of rights, and judicial review — and his views demonstrating some ambivalence toward majority rule in other areas, such as the methods of selection of the chief executive and the members of the legislature. Following this, I will raise some issues concerning the extent to which we know how Mason might apply his views to contemporary issues and the extent to which it is fair to attribute his views to other member of the founding generation.

In considering these matters, we must remember that members of the founding generation had a perspective very different from our own perspective today. Specifically, we must recall that the term "democracy" did not have entirely positive connotations in 1787, at least in part because it was assumed that previous attempts to establish democracies had failed for one reason or another.[20] Indeed, some of the delegates to the 1787 convention were skeptical of the possibility of establishing a successful democracy in a republic as large as one encompassing all of the original colonies.[21]

Views Reflecting an Antagonism Toward Unlimited Majority Rule

There may be a lack of clarity about some issues, but there seems little doubt that George Mason's views belong to the natural law/natural rights tradition — a tradition that finds expression in the writings of Cicero, Coke, and Locke, among others, and that is characterized by the notion that certain principles exist that are independent of and superior to laws enacted by the legislative authority.[22] This tradition is thus inconsistent with the notion of unfettered majority rule as illustrated by the principle of parliamentary supremacy in the United Kingdom.[23]

George Mason's writings and speeches over a twenty-year period consistently demonstrate adherence to this natural law/natural rights tradition. For example, about a year before he drafted a Declaration of Rights for Virginia, he joined the effort to organize a militia to deal with the forthcoming revolt against King George III.[24] While doing so, he addressed certain "remarks on annual elections for the Fairfax Independent Company":

> We came equals into this world, and equals shall we go out of it. All men are by nature born equally free and independent. To protect the weaker from the injuries and insults of the stronger were societies first formed; when men entered into compacts to give up some of their natural rights, that by union and mutual assistance they might secure the rest; but they gave up no more than the nature of the thing required. Every society, all government, and every kind of civil compact therefore, is or ought to be, calculated for the general good and safety of the community.[25]

Similarly, when Mason prepared his first draft of the Virginia Declaration of Rights in May 1776, he included the following:

> That all men are born equally free and independent, and have certain inherent natural Rights, of which they can not by any Compact, deprive or divest their Posterity; among which are the Enjoyment of Life and Liberty, with the Means of acquiring and possessing Property, and pursuing and obtaining Happiness and Safety.
>
> That Power is, by God and Nature, vested in, and consequently derived from the People; that Magistrates are their Trustees and Servants, and at all times amenable to them.[26]

What has already been said indicates that Mason's adherence to the natural law tradition was not restricted to some totally abstract conception; instead, he believed in embodying these principles in a written bill of rights. As noted above, he was the principal author of the Virginia Declaration of Rights, the first bill of rights in America.[27] He also objected to the absence of a bill of rights in the Constitution drafted in Philadelphia in 1787;[28] indeed, the absence of a bill of rights was the was the first deficiency pointed out in his "Objections" to the new Constitution. Although it has been suggested that his real objection was to the compromise between some of the New England states and some of the southern states by which slavery was protected for a time in return for the granting to Congress of the power to control navigation and other commercial matters by simple majority vote,[29] his earlier drafting of the original Virginia Declaration of Rights suggests that his objection to the absence of such a bill of rights from the 1787 Constitution was not a sham.

The next question is whether Mason, a clear believer in the natural law/natural rights tradition and in the notion that there ought to be a written bill of rights, believed that such a bill of rights was merely hortatory or whether he was concerned about actual enforcement of limitations on governmental authority.[30] Today we are likely to think of judicial review as the principal mechanism by which limitations on the majority can be enforced. Other mechanisms, including, of course, various combinations of checks and balances, were discussed during the convention; some of these obviously survived. One that did not survive but which was discussed at some length was the possibility of a council or revision.[31] At one point it was suggested that such a council might consist of the President and members of the Supreme Court. In arguing in favor of such a council of revision, Mason said in part, as reported by Madison:

> Notwithstanding the precautions taken in the Constitution of the Legislature, it would still so much resemble that of the individual States, that it must be expected frequently to pass unjust and pernicious laws. This restraining power was therefore essentially necessary. It would have the effect not only of hindering the final passage of such laws; but would discourage demagogues from attempting to get them passed. It had been said by <Mr. L. Martin> that if the Judges were joined in

this check on the laws, they would have a double negative, since in their expository capacity of Judges they would have one negative. He would reply that in this capacity they could impede in one case only, the operation of laws. They could declare an unconstitutional law void. But with regard to every law however unjust oppressive or pernicious, which did not come plainly under this description, they would be under the necessity as Judges to give it a free course. He wished the further use to be made of the Judges, of giving aid in preventing every improper law. Their aid will be the more valuable as they are in the habit and practice of considering laws in their true principles, and in all their consequences.[32]

At least two observations are pertinent. First, Mason apparently was willing to contemplate having unelected judges exercise, in effect, a veto power over the legislature, at least part of which was to be popularly elected. He accepted the notion of judicial review by stating that the judge "could declare an unconstitutional law void."[33] Second, he wished to go further and give them, along with the executive, power to prevent the passage of laws that were "unjust[,] oppressive[,] or pernicious."[34]

That Mason accepted judicial review is confirmed by some of his arguments during the ratifying convention in Virginia in June 1788. In objecting to the prohibition of the adoption by states of *ex post facto* laws,[35] Mason assumed that the prohibition would include civil laws having a retrospective effect;[36] this prohibition he objected to as being impractical. One of the deleterious effects of having this prohibition, according to Mason, was that "[a]s an expressed power is given to the federal court to take cognizance of such controversies, and to declare null all *ex post facto* laws, I think gentlemen must see there is danger, and that it ought to be guarded against."[37] Here Mason not only accepted the concept of judicial review, but also assumed that the new

Constitution was to embody it.

As previously indicated, Mason objected to granting to Congress the power to enact navigation laws by a simple, rather than by a two-thirds, majority.[38] This objection constitutes very direct evidence of his desire to protect minority rights. He explicitly identified the five southern states as a minority needing protection from the majority of states.[39]

Thus far we have seen a fairly consistent pattern of non acceptance of the principle of unlimited majority rule. Mason's acceptance of the natural law tradition, the concept of a bill of rights, judicial review (or, even more emphatically, a council of revision), and a requirement of a super-majority to pass navigation laws shows not only that he was opposed to unlimited majority rule, but also that he was willing to implement specific measures to insure such limitations.

Views Reflecting an Ambivalence Toward Majority Rule and the Need to Protect Minority Rights

On other issues, Mason's views do not point unambiguously toward insuring majority rule or toward protecting minority rights. Many of these issues involve questions of checks and balances (other than judicial review),[40] the method of selection of various governmental officials, and the terms of office and qualifications of these officials.

Mason did oppose popular election of the chief executive, in part because it seemed impractical to him.[41] He also originally argued for a single seven-year term for the chief executive[42] — a situation that would have frustrated majority rule by making it impossible to select the chief executive for a second term. On the other hand, towards the end of the convention when the issue arose as to the method of selecting the President in the event that a majority of electors did not vote for a single candidate, he favored placing the final choice in the House of Representatives rather than in the Senate because allowing the House to be involved in the selection effected a "lessening [of] the aristocratic influence of the Senate."[43] Mason favored at least part of the provisions of The Great Compromise; that is, he favored popular election of members of the House[44] and election of the Senate by the state legislatures.[45] He argued in favor of property qualifications for the members of the Senate,[46] which presumably would have had anti-democratic consequences; nevertheless, he argued against requiring electors to be freeholders: "Ought the merchant, the monied man, the parent of a number of children whose fortunes are to be pursued in his own Country, to be viewed as suspicious characters, and unworthy to be trusted with the common rights of their fellow Citizens[?]"[47] Also, he argued in favor of ratification of the new constitution by the people rather than by the state legislatures.[48]

With regard to possible limits on legislative action, he again took positions that sometimes favored majority rule and sometimes disfavored it. He argued in favor of giving the House the sole power to originate money bills[49] — a position that presumably favored democracy since the House was to be the more directly representative branch. On the other hand, as already noted, he complained in his "Objections" that a mere majority of the members of the legislature could make "all commercial and navigation laws."[50]

Finally, in discussing the question or the power to tax, he made several general statements expressing his fear of majority tyranny: "He admitted that notwithstanding the superiority of the Republican form over every other, it had its evils. The chief ones, were the danger of the majority oppressing the minority, and the mischievous influence of demagogues."[51]

"He went on a principle often advanced & in which he concurred, that a 'majority when interested will oppress the minority.'"[52]

Present Significance of Mason's Views
If we are to be more than merely historically curious,

we should proceed to ask the question, of what significance are Mason's views for us today? This question seems particularly pertinent in light of Attorney General Meese's announced preference for seeking and presumably implementing the original intention of the framers/ratifiers.[53] This question seems to resolve itself into two subsidiary questions: (a) To what extent can one assume that Mason's views were typical of the opinions of the framers/ratifiers? (b) If we assume, for the sake of argument, that his views were typical of those of many of the framers/ratifiers, to what extent can we look to Mason's views for the resolution of contemporary problems? The answer to both of these questions may depend on whether one asks these questions with reference to particular issues, or whether one asks the question at a fairly high level of generality.

If one focuses on very specific issues, one is frustrated by the disparity of views held by the Anti-Federalists on many subjects. As Herbert Storing put it, "it is not possible to read far among the Anti-Federal writings without being struck by an extraordinary heterogeneity."[54] Of course, what was true of the Anti-Federalists was also true of the Federalists,[55] although the latter did agree at the end of the convention to suppress their individual views.[56]

In short, the Constitution was a compromise among people with widely disparate views on specific issues.[57] In this sense, it may be very difficult to generalize from any one individual's views. On the other hand, if one asks the question at a very high level of generality, the answer may be that Mason shared with his colleagues a good deal.[58] Mason's adherence to natural law was not remarkable at this time; his adherence was totally consistent with the expression of natural law principles by Jefferson in the Declaration of Independence.[59] One can say that in his support of a bill of rights, Mason differed from a majority of the representatives at the 1787 Philadelphia convention;[60] nevertheless, it is clear that there was much sentiment among the various states in the ratifying conventions for a bill of rights,[61] and it was this sentiment, widely shared, that resulted in the proposal for the Bill of Rights in the First Congress of the United States.[62] Since the Bill of Rights was ratified by the requisite number of states (three-quarters of those voting on the subject), it may be reasonable to infer that Mason's views with regard to the necessity of a bill of rights were fairly typical of his day.[63] In regard to the issue of judicial review, although one finds statements of Mason to the effect that some guarantees were to be provided by checks and balances apart from judicial review,[64] it has already been seen that Mason specifically accepted judicial review as a restraint on the legislative authority.[65] Although not discussed at length at the Convention, judicial review was also accepted by other individuals,[66] and was certainly accepted by Hamilton in *The Federalist*,[67] and Madison in his arguments in favor of a bill of rights during the First Congress.[68]

The notion that it may be possible to view Mason as somewhat typical of his generation in regard to very general matters but atypical with regard to specific issues suggests also the difficulty that one may encounter in attempting to look to the "original intention" of the framers/ratifiers in regard to the resolution of issues today. At the highest level of generality, it may be possible to glean from the views of Mason and his contemporaries certain fundamental principles that one may attempt to apply to today's problems. The difficulty with this approach is, of course, that the level of generality[69] is such that one is not likely to receive much guidance in the resolution of specific problems.[70] For example, if one tries to determine the original intention with regard to the possible unconstitutionality of a proposed federal statute to impose the death penalty, one would have to acknowledge, at a high level of abstraction, that Mason and some of his colleagues assumed that the Supreme Court would exercise the power of declaring unconstitutional at least some statutes.[71] At a lower level of abstraction one can say that Mason and his contemporaries assumed that a death penalty provision would pass constitutional muster since the language of the Constitution, as amended by the Bill of Rights, clearly contemplates the existence of capital punishment.[72] The real question, however, may be, how would Mason and his colleagues respond in today's society in which standards of civilized conduct have changed? Given the fact that capital punishment is imposed for many fewer offenses than it was in the late eighteenth century,[73] and in light of changing attitudes towards physical punishments of various kinds, can we say with certainty that Mason today would support capital punishment?[74] We are certainly at liberty to ask the question, but the answer is far from clear.[75]

Similarly, we know that Mason was firmly attached to the principles of free exercise of religion, private property, and the rights of persons accused of crime.[76] He apparently was less concerned about restraints on governmental agents conducting searches.[77] Can we be sure how Mason would respond today in the light of changed circumstances? Would he continue to give a fairly low priority to prohibitions of general searches in light of problems of drug trafficking today?[78] Or, would he be more inclined to treat this principle as fundamental in light of technological change that permit intrusions of a sort utterly unimaginable in 1787?[79]

Questions of this sort are also complicated by subsequent events that unquestionably have changed our constitutional scheme, such as the ratification of the three Civil War amendments[80] (which have altered the fundamental relationship between the federal government and the states) and popular election of senators[81] (which has modified an aspect of the Great Compromise by diminishing the influence of states as states).[82]

One of the issues that arise in regard to state (as contrasted with federal) legislation, of course, is the question of possible incorporation of the provisions of the Bill of Rights into the fourteenth amendment and hence creation of limits on state authority that were not thought to exist in 1787 and 1791.[83] Of course, we cannot ask about Mason's views since he died long before the ratification of this amendment; instead we have to ask questions about the framers/ratifiers of this amendment similar to the questions raised in regard to the framers/ratifiers of the original Constitution. Difficulties of a similar sort arise, including the uncertainty about how they would respond to changed circumstances.[84]

Some persons suggest that if it is not possible to say with certainty that a particular legislative act (whether federal or state) is in conflict with the Constitution, that provision ought to stand.[85] The difficulty with this approach is that as time passes, and with greater technological changes, it becomes harder and harder to say that any particular act of the legislature is in clear conflict with provisions of the Constitution. The result, if one is to accept this view, is to say that virtually any act of the legislature is valid. Thus, a consequence of the pursuit of this approach to constitutional issues is that one places a higher priority on one value of the framers and a lesser priority on another. Specifically, one places a higher value on the statements during the Convention and elsewhere that the courts will strike down only those acts that are clearly contrary to the Constitution,[86] while placing a lower value on the concept of natural rights and the danger of oppression from majority rule — a concept that arguably finds support in the ninth amendment.[87] Who is to say which of these values should be given a higher priority? The framers/ratifiers did not tell us. Even those committed to an adherence to the "original intention" must, therefore, make this judgment for themselves today. If one concludes that the more fundamental principle is protection of minority interests against possible oppression by the majority,[88] one may also conclude that, as a practical matter, the only way to implement this currently is through a considerably more extensive judicial review than was originally anticipated.[89] To the extent that this argument is based on an evolutionary concept of judicial review — that is, one considerably broader than that of the founders — it is perhaps no more objectionable than the evolutionary interpretation of the power of the President as Commander-in-Chief to send United States military forces to fight thousands of miles away from our shores without a congressional declaration of war.[90]

If the analyses contained in this article seem strained because they inevitably reflect our current understanding and thus are not entirely faithful to the spirit of 1787, then perhaps they will serve a useful purpose in illustrating how hard it is to look to the past for the resolution of today's problems.[91]

Summary and Conclusion

George Mason's adherence to the natural law/natural rights tradition, his enthusiasm for bills of rights, and his acceptance of judicial review all place him in opposition to the principle of unfettered majority rule reflected in the British concept of parliamentary supremacy. His views in these areas are fairly typical of those of many of his contemporaries. His positions on more specific issues point less consistently in favor of limits on majority rule; it is also with reference to these more specific issues that his views are less typical of those of the founding generation. Moreover, with the passage of time and changed circumstances (including great technological advances), it becomes very difficult to say how he would resolve many of today's controversial constitutional questions — a point that is probably valid in relation to all the others who participated actively in the great events leading to the founding of the United States.

Footnotes

* Copyright 1987, Board of Regents of Gunston Hall. I am grateful to the Board of Regents of Gunston Hall, which sponsored in large part the research on which this article is based. My thinking on this subject was aided substantially by my attendance at a conference entitled "On the Continued Relevance of the Constitution," held at Claremont McKenna College from June 16 to July 2, 1986, sponsored by the National Endowment for the Humanities, and co-directed by Lino Graglia and Ralph Rossum. I wish also to thank John Kaminski, Director of the Center for the Study of the American Constitution, University of Wisconsin, for permitting me to examine the files compiled by him and his colleagues as part of the project entitled "The Documentary History of the Ratification of the Constitution and the Bill of Rights." I am indebted also to Josephine Pacheco, Department of History, George Mason University, who read a draft of this article. The views expressed in this article are my own and not necessarily those of any sponsoring organization or other individual, and I am, of course, solely responsible for any errors contained herein.

**Professor of Law, George Mason University. A.B., Dartmouth College; J. D., University of Michigan; LL.M., Harvard University; J.S.D., Columbia University.

1. This biographical note is based primarily on H. Miller, *George Mason, Gentleman Revolutionary* (1975); R. Rutland, *George Mason and the War for Independence* (1976); *The Papers of George Mason* (R. Rutland ed. 1970) [hereinafter *Mason*]. Other biographies of Mason include P. Copeland & R. McMaster, *The Five George Masons: Patriots and Planters of Maryland and Virginia* (1975); F. Henri, *George Mason of Virginia* (1971); H. Miller, *George Mason of Gunston Hall* (1958); H. Miller, *George Mason, Constitutionalist* (1938); K. Rowland, *The Life of George Mason* (1892); and R. Rutland, *George Mason, Reluctant Statesman* (1961).

2. He served on the Fairfax County Court from 1747 to 1752 and from 1764 to 1789. His record of attendance, however, was not good; indeed, "[n]o other justice surpassed his record of nonattendance." Horrell, George Mason and the Fairfax Court, 91 *Va. Mag. Hist & Biography* 418, 422 (1983).

3. "This is, to be sure, a very old problem – as old as government itself: it is a universal problem, pressing everywhere for solution." H. Commager, Majority Rule and Minority Rights 4 (1958). The tension exists particularly whenever some form of democracy operates. In the pure democracy of ancient Athens, for example, the tension was largely resolved by permitting the majority to dominate whatever minority or minorities might have existed. This is not to say, however, that no restraints existed. Despite the fact that the whole people made basic policy decisions, it was still necessary to have some governmental officials implement these policies. These governmental officials were largely chosen by lot. *See generally* 4 G. Grote, *A History of Greece* 438-86 (1888); J. Mosley, Election by Lot a Athens 145-53 (1933). Because they were selected by lot and served for brief periods (perhaps only a year), they were presumably constrained in their actions by the realization that shortly they would return to the general population and be subject to the control, at least in part, of their fellow citizens. This awareness presumably caused them to be careful about not offending individuals who later would have substantial control over them.

4. Much of President Roosevelt's New Deal legislation was obviously representative of this particular approach. *See*, e.g., R. Moley, *The First New Deal* (1966).

5. This defense of property rights took the form, traditionally, of decisions striking down state statutes imposing limitations on employers – e.g., Lochner v. New York, 198 U.S. 45 (1905), in which the Supreme Court invalidated a state statute limiting employment in bakeries to 60 hours a week and 10 hours a day – and congressional efforts to deal with the many problems created by the Great Depression. *See*, e.g., Schechter Poultry Corp. v. United States, 295 U.S. 495 (1935). In *Lochner*, the Court, although insisting that :[t]his is not a question of substituting the judgment of the court for that of the legislature," nevertheless invalidated the limitation on the hours of work for bakers, concluding in part:
> It is impossible for us to shut our eyes to the fact that many of the laws of this character, while passed under what is claimed to be the police power for the purpose of protecting the public health or welfare, are, in reality, passed from other motives. We are justified in saying so when, from the character of the law and the subject on which it legislates, it is apparent that public health or welfare bears but the most remote relation to the law. *Lochner*, 198 U.S. at 56-57.
>
> It seems to us that the real object and purpose were simply to regulate the hours of labor between the master and his employés (all being men,

sui juris) in a private business, not dangerous in any degree to morals or any real and substantial degree, to the health of the employés. Under such circumstances the freedom of master and employé to contract with each other in relation to their employment, and in defining the same, cannot be prohibited or interfered with, without violating the Federal Constitution. *Id.* at 64.

6. Compare, *e.g.*, H. Commager, *Majority Rule and Minority Rights* (1958) with H. Commager, Freedom and Order: A Commentary on the American Political Scene 3-51 (1966).

7. Graglia, How the Constitution Disappeared, *Commentary*, Feb. 1986, at 19. Only under very rare circumstances would Graglia permit judicial review. See *infra* note 85. Is it proper to view Graglia as an ideological descendant, for example, of Justices Butler and McReynolds? In at least one area I believe that the answer is a qualified yes. Certainly Lino Graglia has in common with Justices Pierce Butler and James C McReynolds and lack of sympathy for persons accused of crime. See Powell v. Alabama, 287 U.S. 45, 73 (1932) (Butler, J., dissenting) (late and uncertain appointment of counsel in capital case should not require reversal, despite contrary views of majority including Sutherland and Van Devanter, JJ.) In other areas, the answer is less clear, in part because many of the current controversial issues, such as abortion, school prayer, and busing to achieve racial balance, did not come before the Court when Justice Butler sat.

Chief Justice Rehnquist may be an even closer ideological descendant of Justices Butler and McReynolds. While deferring to the legislature in the area of individual rights – see, *e.g.*, Furman v. Georgia, 408 U.S. 238, 465-70 (1972) (Rehnquist, J., dissenting) (disagreeing with conclusion that death penalty as then administered violated prohibition of cruel and unusual punishment) – he has been willing on occasion to strike down legislation that, in his view, has interfered with property rights. For instance, he was part of the majority in *Allied Structural Steel Co. v. Spannaus*, 438 U.S. 234 (1978), and United State Trust Co. v. New Jersey, 431 U.S. 1 (1977), two cases in which the Court struck down state statutes under the contracts clause (U.S. Const. art. I, § 10, cl. 1). Attorney General Meese's approach seems very similar to that of Chief Justice Rehnquist. See *infra* note 12. One of the most radical modern defenses of private property is found in the writings of Richard Epstein. See, *e.g.*, R. Epstein, *Takings: Private Property and the Power of Eminent Domain* (1985). Epstein acknowledges that his approach is founded at least in part on the theory of natural rights. *Id.* at 5.

8. The Virginia Declaration of Rights of 1776 went through three drafts, the first of which is in George Mason's handwriting, except for the last several paragraphs, which are in the handwriting of Thomas Ludwell Lee. For a full discussions of Mason's role, see 1 Mason, *supra* note 1, at 279-82, 285-86, 289-91.

9. 3 Mason, *supra* note 1, at 885-994.

10. *Id.* at 1047-1120.

11. The importance of values in the determination of one's attitudes towards specific objects or issues is discussed at some length in M. Rokeach, *The Nature of Human Values* (1973).

12. Attorney General Meese has argued that the "principle of separation of powers contributes to the preservation and perpetuation of individual liberty." Address by Attorney General Edwin Meese III, Bicentennial Program of the University of Dallas, in Irving, Texas (Feb. 27, 1986). This argument, combined with his advocacy of a return to a "jurisprudence of original intention," would lead to a lesser role for the Supreme Court. At the same time, however, he has criticized the Supreme Court for

refusing to strike down the effort on the part of Congress to apply the Fair Labor Standards Act to public mass transportation systems, as in *San Antonio Garcia v. San Antonio Metro. Transit Auth.*, 469 U.S. 528 (1985). In particular, of course, Meese has been displeased that the Court in *Garcia* overturned a prior case, *National League of Cities v. Usery*, 426 U.S. 833 (1976), and in the process indicated that it would not interfere with the decisions of Congress in this area. Address by Attorney General Edwin Meese III, American Bar Association (July 9, 1985), reprinted in *The Federalist Society, The Great Debate: Interpreting Our Written Constitution* 1, 3-4 (Occasional Paper No. 2, 1986).

13. The concept of "selective perception," which involves differing perceptions of the "same" transaction or event based on differing backgrounds, purposes, beliefs, attitudes, and values is well known to psychology. See Hastorf & Cantril, The Saw a Game: A Case Study, 49 J. *Abnormal & Social Psychology* 129 (1954); Vidmar & Rokeach, Archie Bunker's Bigotry: A Study in Selective Perception and Exposure, 24 *J. Comm.* 36 (1974).

14. Establishment of the original government under the Constitution of 1787 required ratification by conventions in 9 of the 13 colonies (U.S. Const. art. VII); subsequent amendments are valid when ratified by legislatures or conventions in three-quarter of the states. U.S. Const. art V. Hamilton, in *The Federalist*, argued in favor of judicial review on the assumption that such review would protect majority rule (the rule pronounced by the super-majority at the time of ratification) as against later legislative majorities, which were assumed not to reflect the will of the people in the same sense in which the original constitution would. *The Federalist* No. 78 at 525 (A. Hamilton)(J. Cooke ed. 1961).

15. The criticism of judicial review as an anti-majoritarian process certainly assumes that judicial review frustrates the will of the present majority. See, e.g., A. Bickel, *The Least Dangerous Branch: The Supreme Court at the Bar of Politics* 16-17 (1962):

> The root difficulty is that judicial review is a counter-majoritarian force in our system. There are various ways of sliding over this ineluctable reality. Marshall did so when he spoke of enforcing, in behalf of "the people," the limits that they have ordained for the institutions of a limited government. And it has been done ever since in much the same fashion by all too many commentators. Marshall himself followed Hamilton, who in the 78th *Federalist* denied that judicial review implied a superiority of the judicial over the legislative power – denied, in other words, that judicial review constituted control by an unrepresentative minority of an elected majority. "It only supposes," Hamilton went on, "that the power of the people is superior to both; and that where the will of the legislature declared in its statutes, stands in opposition to that of the people, declared in the Constitution, the judges ought to be governed by the latter rather than the former." But the word "people" so used is an abstraction. Not necessarily a meaningless or a pernicious one by any means; always charged with emotion, but nonrepresentational – an abstraction obscuring the reality that when the Supreme Court declares unconstitutional a legislative act or the action of an elected executive, it thwarts the will of representatives of the actual people of the here and now; it exercises control, not in behalf of the prevailing majority, but against it. That, without mystic overtones, is what actually happens. It is an altogether different kettle of fish, and it is the reason the charge can be made that judicial review is undemocratic.

16. For example, during a discussion of a clause providing that bills raising money

had to originate in the House, Mason admitted that "notwithstanding the superiority of the Republican form over every other, it had its evils. The chief ones, were the danger of the majority oppressing the minority, and the mischievous influence of demagogues." J. Madison, *Notes of Debates in the Federal Convention of 1787*, at 443 (A. Koch rev. ed. 1985) [hereinafter *Madison's Notes*].

17. Mr. Wilson considered the election of the 1st branch by the people not only as the corner stone, but as the foundation of the fabric: and that the difference between a mediate & immediate election was immense. The difference was particularly worthy of notice in this respect: that the Legislatures are actuated not merely by the sentiment of the people; but have an official sentiment opposed to that of the Genl. Govt. and perhaps to that of the people themselves. *Madison's Notes, supra* note 16, at 167.

Later Madison expressed views more similar to those of Mason (see *supra* note 16) than to those of Wilson:

Whenever the real power in a Government lies, there is the danger of oppression. In our Governments the real power lies in the majority of the Community, and the invasion of private rights, is *chiefly* to be apprehended, not from acts of Government contrary to the sense of its constituents, but from acts in which the Government is the mere instrument of the major number of the constituents. Letter from James Madison to Thomas Jefferson (Oct. 17, 1788), reprinted in 11 *The Papers of James Madison* 298 (R. Rutland & C. Hobson ed. 1977) (emphasis in original) [hereinafter *Papers of James Madison*].

18. There remains, of course, the debate over whether representatives are simply to act as their constituents presently would act, or whether they should look beyond the passions of the moment to secure the long term public good. See, e.g., M. Edelman, *Democratic Theories and the Constitution* 15-16 (1984).

19. Despite the electoral college (U.S. Const. art II, § 1, cl. 2; U.S. Const. amend XII), the President is still assumed to be broadly representative of the people: "[I]t is fair to say that the American presidency does represent a majority of the people and comes closer to the majoritarian ideal that practically any other national office in the modern western democracies" J Choper, *Judicial Review and the National Political Process* 47 (1980). Certainly President Reagan, in pressing Congress to adopt his budget proposals, has assumed that he represents the people as a whole. See, e.g., *N.Y. Times*, June 17, 1981, § 1, at 26, col. 1.

20. Madison said, for example: "In Greece & Rome the rich & poor, the creditors & debtors, as well as the patricians & plebeians alternately oppressed each other with equal unmercifulness," *Madison's Notes, supra* note 16, at 76. In discussing the problem of faction, Madison also said:

When a majority is included in a faction, the form of popular government on the other hand enables it to sacrifice to its ruling passion or interest, both the public gook, and the rights of other citizens. To secure the public good, and private rights, against the danger of such a faction, and at the same time preserve the spirit and the form of popular government, is then the great object to which our enquiries are directed: Let me add that it is the great desideratum, by which alone this form of government can be rescued from the opprobrium under which it has so long labored, and be recommended to the esteem and adoption of mankind. *The Federalist* No. 10, at 60-61 (J. Madison)(J. Cooke ed. 1961).

21. Independent of the opinions of many great authors that a free

elective government cannot be extended over large territories, a few reflections must evince, that one government and general legislation alone, never can extend equal benefits to all parts of the United States: Deferent laws, customes, and opinions exist in the different states, which by a uniform system of laws would be unreasonably invaded. The United States contain about a million square miles, and in half a century will, probably contain ten millions of people; and from the center to the extremes is about 800 miles. Letter from *Federal Farmer* (Oct. 8, 1787), reprinted in *The Anti-Federalist* 39 (H. Storing ed. 1981, abr. M. Dry 1985).

22. See generally Corwin, The "Higher Law" Background of American Constitutional Law, 42 Harv. L. Rev. 149, 365 (1928, 1929); J. Stone, *Human Law and Human Justice* 1-104 (1965).

23. "[Parliamentary sovereignty] means first, that all legislative power within the realm is vested in Parliament, or is derived from the authority of Parliament – Parliament thus has no rival within the legislative sphere – and it means secondly that there is no legal limit to the power of Parliament." P. James, *Introduction to English Law* 8 (10th ed. 1979).

24. Even before his involvement in the militia, Mason participated in the preparation of the Fairfax County Resolves, in which the "freeholders and inhabitants of the county of Fairfax" set forth certain grievances against the British Crown. The natural law foundation upon which this document rests is illustrated by the following:

That our Ancestors, when they left their native Land, and settled in America brought with them (even if the same had not been confirmed by Charters) the Civil Constitution and Form of Government of the Country they came from; and were by the Laws of Nature and Nations, and entitled to all it's Privileges, Immunities and Advantages, which have descended to us their Posterity, and ought of Right to be as fully enjoyed, as if we had still continued within the Realm of England. 1 *Mason, supra* note 1, at 201.

25. *Id.* at 229.

26. *Id.* at 277. See also *id.* at 434-35; 2 *Mason, supra* note 1, at 695, 697, 706, 741, 751. 766, 768, 770, 771, 774, 776, 780, 811, 860, 862; 3 *Mason, supra* note 2, at 84, 85, 1164, 1177, 1189, 1199, 1203-04, 1214, 1220, 1221.

27. See *supra* note 8.

28. 3 *Mason, supra* note 1, at 991.

29. See D. Ellsworth, Letters of "A Landholder," in *Essays on the Constitution of the United States* 161-62 (P. Ford ed. 1982).

30. In a seminar entitled "On the Continued Relevance of the Constitution," sponsored by the National Endowment for the Humanities, held at Claremont McKenna College between June 16 and July 2, 1986, Lino Graglia, one of the co-directors, took the view that the Bill of Rights is largely a statement of principles not necessarily to be enforced.

31. A "council of revision" was first proposed in para. 8 of the resolutions proposed by Edmond Randolph on May 29, 1787 (the Virginia Plan). *Madison's Notes, supra* note 16, at 32.

32. 3 *Mason, supra* note 1, at 928.

33. *Id.*

34. *Id.*

35. U.S. Const. art. I, § 10.

36. Mason had expressed a similar view during the convention in Philadelphia in

1787. *Mason, supra* note 1, at 986-87. His view was contrary to that of Mr. Dickenson, *Madison's Notes, supra* not 16, at 547. Following ratification, the United States Supreme Court resolved the question by deciding that the *ex post facto* prohibition was limited to criminal statutes *Calder* v. *Bull*, 3 U.S. (3 Dall.) 386 (1798).
37. 3 *Mason, supra* note 1, at 1091.
38. *Id*. at 992.
39. *Id*.
40. For the view that Madison regarded checks and balances (together with the division of power between the central government and the states, and the multiplicity of interests in an extended republic) as the chief guarantee against majority tyranny, see Rossum, "To Render These Rights Secure": James Madison's Understanding of the Relationship of the Constitution to the Bill of Rights, 3 *Benchmark* 4 (1987).
41. 3 *Mason, supra* note 1, at 925.
42. *Id*. at 894.
43. *Id*. at 977.
44. *Id*. at 888, 900, 910.
45. *Id*. at 902, 915-16.
46. *Id*. at 916-17.
47. *Id*. at 949-50.
48. *Id*. at 929.
49. *Id*. at 921, 951, 952, 955-56, 958.
50. *Id*. at 992. See *supra* text accompanying note 29.
51. *Id*. at 956.
52. *Id*. at 965.
53. "It has been and will continue to be the policy of this administration to press for a Jurisprudence of Original Intention." Speech by Edwin Meese III, before the American Bar Association (July 9, 1985), reprinted in *The Federalist Society, The Great Debate Interpreting Our Written Constitution* 1, 10 (Occasional Paper No. 2, 1986).
54. H. Storing, *What the Anti-Federalists Were For* 5 (1981).
55. "There were in fact diverse and contradictory opinions among the Federalists just as there were among their opponents." *Id*.
56. That they continued to have differences but agreed to suppress them for the common good, is suggested by Franklin's memorable speech at the close of the convention, in which he said, among other things:

> I confess that there are several parts of this constituents which I do not at present approve, but I am not sure I shall never approve them...I doubt too whether any other Convention we can obtain, may be able to make a better Constitution. For when you assemble a number of men to have the advantage of their joint wisdom, you inevitably assemble with those men, all their prejudices, their passions, their errors of opinion, their local interests, and their selfish views. From such an assembly can a perfect production be expected? It therefore astonishes me, Sir, to find this system approaching so near to perfection as it does; and I think it will astonish our enemies, who are waiting with confidence to hear that our councils are confounded like those of the Builders of Babel; and that our States are on the point of separation, only to meet hereafter for the purpose of cutting one another's throat's throats. Thus I consent, Sir, to this Constitution because I expect no better, and because I am not sure, that it is not the best. The opinions I have had of its errors, I sacrifice to the public good. I have never whispered a syllable of them abroad. Within these walls they were born, and here they shall die. If every one

of us in returning to our Constituents were to report the objections he has had to it, and endeavor to gain partisans in support of them, we might prevent its being generally received, and thereby lose all the salutary effects & great advantages resulting naturally in our favor among foreign Nations as well as among ourselves, from our real or apparent unanimity. *Madison's Notes, supra* note 16, at 653-54.

57. The extremes are illustrated by Patterson's plan, which would have created a national executive and judiciary, by which otherwise would have amended the Articles of Confederation only slightly (*id.* at 118-21, and by Hamilton's proposal, which would, in effect, have abolished the states and created a national government in which the members of the upper house and the chief executive would have served for life. *Id.* at 138-39.

58. If the Federalists and Anti-Federalists were divided among themselves, they were, at a deeper level, united with one another. Their disagreements were not based on different premises about the nature of man or the ends of political life. They were not the deep cleavages of contending regimes. They were the much less sharp and clear-cut differences within the family, as it were, of men agreed that the purpose of government is the regulation and thereby the protection of individual rights and that the best instrument for this purpose is some form of limited, republican government. *Storing, supra* note 54, at 5.

59. Though authored in the first instance by Jefferson, the Declaration of Independence was, of course, approved in amendment form by Congress, and thus may be said to reflect commonly held views. See T. Jefferson, Notes of Proceedings in the Continental Congress, in *The Papers of Thomas Jefferson* 314-19 (J. Boyd ed. 1956).

60. On September 12, 1787, following Mason's suggestion, Gerry "moved for a Committee to prepare a Bill of Rights." Voting by states, the delegates defeated the motion by a vote of 10 to 0, with Massachusetts abstaining. *Madison's Notes, supra* note 16, at 616, 630.

61. Evidence of this is abundant. For example, the ratification statements from Massachusetts, New Hampshire, Virginia, and New York explicitly referred to the need for amendments to the Constitution; North Carolina finally ratified in 1790 following an initial refusal to ratify until amendments were adopted. 1 *The Debates in the Several Conventions on the Adoption of the Constitution* 318-33 (J. Elliot ed. 1836).

62. I will state my reasons why I think it proper to propose amendments, and state the amendments themselves, so far as I think they ought to be proposed. If I thought I could fulfil the duty which I owe to myself and my constituents, to let the subject pass over in silence, I most certainly should not trespass upon the indulgence of this House. But I cannot do this and am therefore compelled to beg a patient hearing to what I have to lay before you And I do most sincerely believe, that if Congress will devote but one day to this subject so far as to satisfy the public that we do not disregard their wishes, it will have a salutory influence on the public councils, and prepare the way for a favorable reception of our future measures. It appears to me that this House is bound by every motive of prudence not to let the first session pass over without proposing to the State Legislatures some things to be incorporated into the constitution, that will render it as acceptable to the whole people of the United States, as it has been found acceptable to a majority of them I wish among other reasons why something should be

done, that those who have bee friendly to the adoption of this constitution may have the opportunity of proving to those who were opposed to it that they were as sincerely devoted to liberty and a Republican Government as those who charged them with wishing the adoption of this constitution in order to have the foundation of an aristocracy or despotism. It will be a desirable thing to extinguish from the bosom of every member of the community, any apprehensions that there are those among his countrymen who wish to deprive them of the liberty for which they valiantly fought and honorably bled. And if there are amendments desired of such a nature as will not injure the constitution, and they can be ingrafted so as to give satisfaction to the doubting part of our fellow-citizens, the friends of the Federal Government will evince that spirit of deferrence and concession for which they have hitherto been distinguished.

It cannot be a secret to the gentlemen in this House, that, notwithstanding the ratification of this system of Government by eleven of the thirteen United States, in some cases unanimously, in others by large majorities; yet still there is a great number of our constituents who are dissatisfied with it; among whom are many respectable for their talents and patriotism, and respectable for the jealousy they have for their liberty, which, though mistaken in its object, is laudable in its motive. There is a great body of the people falling under this description, who at present feel much inclined to join their support to the cause of Federalism, if they were satisfied on this one point. We ought not to disregard their inclination, but, on principles of amity and moderation, we conform to their wishes, and expressly declare the great rights of mankind secured under this constitution. 1 *Annals of Cong.* 448-49 (J. Gales ed. 1789) (statement of James Madison).

63. It is well accepted as a matter of statutory construction, for example, that amendments of a stature that are required in order to get the assent of a particular portion of the legislature and thus to assure passage of a particular bill accurately reflect the purpose to be attributed to the legislature. See, *e.g.*, Thornburg v. Gingles, 106 S. Ct. 2752, 2784 (1986) (O'Connor, J., concurring in the judgment).

64. His support for a council of revision was an instance of an effort to provide a check on the legislative tendency to pass "unjust and pernicious laws." 3 *Mason, supra* note 1, at 928.

65. See *supra* note 32 and accompanying text.

66. It seems fairly clear, for example, that Gerry, Martin, and Gouverneur Morris supported judicial review. *Madison's Notes, supra* note 16, at 61, 340, 463. Mercer and Dickenson spoke against it. *Id.* at 462-63. For a discussion of the extent to which the Founders supported the notion of judicial review at the time of the Philadelphia convention in 1787, see, e.g., Levy, Judicial Review, History, and Democracy: An Introduction, in *Judicial Review in the Supreme Court: Selected Essays* 2-6 (L. Levy ed. 1967).

67. The complete independence of the courts of justice is peculiarly essential in a limited constitution. By a limited constitution I understand one which contains certain specified exceptions to the legislative authority: such for instance as that it shall pass no bills of attainder, no *ex post facto* laws, and the like, Limitations of this kind can be preserved in practice no other way than through the medium of the courts of justice; whose duty it must be to declare all acts contrary to the manifest

tenor of the constitution void. Without this, all the reservations of particular rights or privileges would amount to nothing. *The Federalist* No. 78, at 524 (A. Hamilton) (J. Cooke ed. 1961).

According to Leonard Levy, this statement is "evidence of shrewd political tactics, not the framers' intention to vest judicial review in the Supreme Court over acts of Congress." *Levy, supra* note 66, at 6.

68.   If they [the Articles of Amendment] are incorporated into the constitution, independent tribunals of justice will consider themselves in a peculiar manner the guardians of those rights; they will be an impenetrable bulwark against every assumption of power in the legislative or executive; they will be naturally led to resist every encroachment upon rights expressly stipulated for in the constitution by the declaration of rights. 12 *Papers of James Madison, supra* note 17, at 206-07.

Levy has remarked, however, on "how treacherous is any generalization about [Madison's] commitment to judicial review." *Levy, supra* note 66, at 4. Those who claim that Madison only later and reluctantly became a champion of judicial review must take into account the following statement that Madison made during the convention in Philadelphia in 1787: "A law violating a treaty ratified by a pre-existing law, might be respected by the Judges as a law, though an unwise or perfidious one. A law violating a constitution established by the people themselves, would be considered by the Judges as null & void." *Madison's Notes, supra* note 16, at 352-53.

69.   On the question whether one interpreting the Constitution is constrained in choosing the appropriate level of generality, compare Brest, The Fundamental Rights Controversy: The Essential Contradictions of Normative Constitutional Scholarship, 90 *Yale* L.J. 1063, 1091-92 (1981)("all adjudication requires making choices among the levels of generality on which to articulate principles, and all such choices are inherently non-neutral") with Address by Judge Bork at the University of San Diego Law School (Nov. 18, 1985), reprinted in *The Federalist Society. The Great Debate: Interpreting Our Written Constitution* 43, 48 (Occasional Paper No. 2, 1986)("I think that ... an intentionalist can do what Brest says be cannot.") For an illustration of Bork's choice of one of three levels of generality in the fourth amendment area, see Bork, Introduction to G. McDowell, *The Constitution and Contemporary Constitutional Theory* at X (Center for Judicial Studies, Constitutional Commentary No. 3, 1985).

70.   See, *e.g.*, R. Unger, Knowledge and Politics 78 (1975)("the proponents of objective value must restrict themselves to a few abstract ideas whose vagueness allows almost any interpretation").

71.   See *supra* note 32 and accompanying text.

72.   The fifth amendment refers to "a capital" crime, being placed "in jeopardy of life," and to being "deprived of life." U.S. Const. amend. V.

73.   Consider, for example, the following excerpt from a statute dealing with bigamy, passed by the Virginia legislature in 1788:

Whereas it hath been doubted whether bigamy or polygamy be punishable by the laws of this commonwealth; *Be it enacted by the General Assembly*, that if any person or persons within this commonwealth, being married, or who shall hereafter marry, do at any time after the first day of February, which shall be in the year of our Lord, one thousand seven hundred and eighty-nine, marry any person or persons, the former husband or wife, being alive, that then every such offense shall be felony, and the person or persons, so offending, shall suffer death as in cases of felony... 12 *Henning's Statutes at Large* (Va. 691 (1823) (emphasis in original).

As indicated in the last portion of the above-quoted statute, "[u]nder the English common law all felonies were punished by death except that the penalty for mayhem was mutilation." R. Perkins & R. Boyce, *Criminal Law* 14 (3rd ed. 1982).

74. Would Mason, for example, take the approach that the Supreme Court took over 40 years before Earl Warren became Chief Justice when in Weems v. United States, 217 U.S. 349 (1910), it struck down as violative of the prohibition against cruel and unusual punishment, a punishment of fifteen years of "cadena" was described by the Court as follows:

> [C]onfinement in a penal institution...a chain at the ankle, and wrist of the offender, hard and painful labor, no assistance from friend or relative, no marital authority or parental rights of property, no participation even in the family council. These parts of this penalty endure for the term of imprisonment. From other parts there is no intermission. His prison bars and chains are removed, it is true, after [15] years, but he goes from them to a perpetual limitation of his liberty. He is forever kept within the shadow of his crime, forever kept within voice and view of the criminal magistrate, not being able to change his domicile without giving notice to the authority immediately in charge of his surveillance, and without permission in writing. *Id.* at 366.

In striking down this provision, the Court stated:

> Legislation, both statutory and constitutional, is enacted, it is true, from an experience of evils, but its general language should not, therefore, be necessarily confined to the form that evil had theretofore taken. Time works changes, brings into existence new conditions and purposes. Therefore a principle to be vital must be capable of wider application than the mischief which gave it birth. This is peculiarly true of constitutions. They are not ephemeral enactments, designed to meet passing occasions. They are, to use the words of Chief Justice Marshall, 'designed to approach immortality as nearly as human institutions can approach it.' The future is their care and provision for events of good and bad tendencies of which no prophecy can be made. In the application of a constitution, therefore, our contemplation cannot be only of what has been but of what may be. Under any other rule a constitution would indeed be as easy of application as it would be deficient in efficacy and power. Its general principles would have little value and be converted by precedent into impotent and lifeless formulas. Rights declared in words might be lost in reality. *Id.* at 373.

75. Presumably it is the difficulty of ascertaining how the Founders would apply general principles to present-day conditions that led Justice Brennan to describe Attorney General Meese's approach as "arrogance cloaked as humility." Address by Justice Brennan, Georgetown University Teaching Symposium (Oct. 1985), reprinted in *The Federalist Society, The Great Debate: Interpreting Our Constitution* 11, 14 (Occasional Paper No. 2, 1986). The uncertainties are not limited merely to the question of how one of the Founders might approach a particular problem today. The ambiguity of the notion of "original intent" includes the question whether the Founders thought that the courts, in interpreting the Constitution, would look to the Founders' understanding of the meaning of the words, as opposed to something else, such as "the plain meaning" of the words themselves. At least one writer has concluded that the Framers did not expect that courts would apply Meese's notion of the original intention of the Framers. Powell, The Original Understanding of Original Intent, 98 *Har. L. Rev.* 885 (1985). Paul Brest has identified at least four approaches

that might be included within the notion of a search for original intent: "strict originalism" (which itself can be broken down into "strict textualism" and "strict intentionalism") and "moderate originalism" (which can also be broken down into "moderate textualism" and "moderate intentionalism"). Brest, The Misconceived Quest for the Original Understanding, 60 *B.U.L. Rev.* 204, 204-05 (1980).

76. The following passages from Mason's first draft from the Virginia Declaration of Rights are illustrative:

> That all men are born equally free and independent, and have certain inherent natural rights, of which they can not by any Compact, deprive or divest their Posterity: among which are the Enjoyment of Life and Liberty, with the Means of acquiring and possessing Property, and pursuing and obtaining Happiness and Safety...
>
> That in all capital or criminal prosecutions, a Man hath a right to demand the Cause and Nature of his Accusation, to be confronted with the Accusers or Witnesses, to call for Evidence in his favor, and to a speedy Trial by jury of his Vicinage; without whose unanimous Consent, he can not be found guilty; nor can he be compelled to give Evidence against himself. And that no Man, except in times of actual Invasion or Insurrection, can be imprisoned upon Suspicion of Crimes against the State, unsupported by Legal Evidence...
>
> That as Religion, or the Duty which we owe to our divine and omnipotent Creator, and the Manner of discharging it, can be governed only by Reason and Conviction, not by Force or Violence; and therefore that all Men shou'd enjoy the fullest Toleration in the Exercise of Religion, according to the Dictates of Conscience, unpunished and unrestrained by the Magistrate, unless, under Colour of Religion, any man disturb the Peace, the Happiness, or Safety of Society, or of Individuals. And that it is the mutual Duty of all, to practice Christian Forbearance, Love and Charity, towards Each other. 1 *Mason, supra* note 1, 277-79.

77. The provision in the first draft of the Virginia Declaration of Rights dealing with general warrants is in Thomas Ludwell Lee's handwriting; it contains the phrase "another [alteration] is agreed to in committee." *Id.* at 278. It thus appears possible that Mason viewed restraints on officials' searching property as less important than other restraints on government. This possibility is strengthened by his later reference to an amended version of this clause as "not of fundamental nature." *Id.* at 286.

78. Consider, for example, the approach taken by Justice Blackmun in Florida v. Royer, 460 U.S. 491, 513 (1983) (Blackmun, J., dissenting), in which he disagreed that probable cause was required before certain restraints were placed upon the defendant: "In my view, the police conduct in this case was minimally intrusive. Given the strength of society's interest in overcoming the extraordinary obstacles to the detection of drug traffickers, such conduct should not be subjected to a requirement of probable cause. Because the Court holds otherwise, I dissent."

79. It was, of course, sensitivity to the degree of intrusiveness permitted by technological change that caused the Court in Katz v. United States, 389 U.S. 347 (1967), to decide that the act of attaching a listening device to the outside of a glass telephone booth constituted a violation of the fourth amendment despite the fact that there was no physical intrusion (and hence no trespass) and despite the fact that, on the face of it, it would be difficult to say that conversations were "persons, houses, papers, [or] effects." U.S. Const. amend. IV.

80. The thirteenth amendment (1865) prohibits slavery; the fourteenth (1868)

restrains the states, *inter alia*, through the due process and equal protection clauses; the fifteenth (1870) forbids racial discrimination in voting. All three amendments grant Congress the power to enforce these amendments "by appropriate legislation." U.S. Const., amend., XIII, § 2; amend. XIV, § 5; amend. XV, § 2.

81. The seventeenth amendment, providing that Senators are to be "elected by the People" of the states that they represent, was ratified in 1913. U.S. Const. amend. XVII, § 1.

82. Recall the Great Compromise entailed popular election (and proportionate representation) in the House and equal representation in the Senate, with Senators being chosen by their respective state legislatures. *Madison's Notes, supra* note 16, at 380, 382.

83. A number of theories have been utilized by the United States Supreme Court, or by members of that Court, to explain how principles found in the Bill of Rights apply to the states by members of that Court, to explain how principles found in the Bill of Rights apply to the states by virtue of the fourteenth amendment. Justice Cardozo, for example, applied a "fundamental fairness" approach under which governmental restraints "implicit in the concept of ordered liberty" were applied to the states under the due process clause of the fourteenth amendment (Palko v. Connecticut, 302 U.S. 319, 325 (1937)); under this approach federal precedents are not automatically binding on the states. Justice Black viewed the whole Bill of Rights as totally incorporated into § 1 of the fourteenth amendment (*e.g.*, Adamson v. California, 332 U.S. 46, 71-72 (1947)(Black, J., dissenting)); this approach requires application of federal precedents to state cases. Two similar approaches have been advocated. "Total incorporation plus" was championed by Justices Murphy and Rutledge, who followed Black, except that, unlike Black, they did not view the fourteenth amendment as limited to the rights specifically enumerated in the Bill of Rights. *Id.* at 124 (Murphy, J. dissenting). Finally, "selective incorporation" has been accepted by a majority of the Supreme Court for the past 25 years; this approach is similar to Black's except that a few provisions, most notably the seventh amendment (jury trial in civil cases) and the grand jury guarantee of the fifth amendment, have not been incorporated because they have not been deemed fundamental in the Anglo-American system of jurisprudence. Duncan v. Louisiana 391 U.S. 145 (1968).

84. Reargument was largely devoted to the circumstances surrounding the adoption of the Fourteenth Amendment in 1868. It covered exhaustively consideration of the Amendment in Congress, ratification by the states, then existing practices and racial segregation and the views of proponents and opponents of the Amendment. This discussion and our own investigation convince us that, although the sources cast some light, it is not enough to resolve the problem with which we are faced. At best they are inconclusive. The most avid proponents of the post-War Amendments undoubtedly intended them to remove all legal distinctions among "all persons born or naturalized in the United States. Their opponents just as certainly, were antagonistic to both the letter and spirit of the Amendments and wished them to have the most limited effect. What others in Congress and the state legislatures had in mind cannot be determined with any degree of certainty. Brown v. Board of Education, 347, U.S. 483, 489 (1954).

Today, education is perhaps the most important function of state and local governments...Today it is a principal instrument in awakening the child to cultural values and preparing him for the latter professional training, and in helping him to adjust normally to his environment. In these days it is doubtful that any child may reasonably be expected to succeed in life if he is denied the opportunity of an education. Such an opportunity where the state has undertaken to provide it, is a right which must be made available to all on equal terms. *Id.* at 493.

85. This view is implicit in Graglia, *supra* note 7, at 19-27. This point was made explicit during the seminar entitled "On the Continued Relevance of the Constitution, sponsored by the National Endowment for the Humanities, held between June 16 and July 2, 1986, at Claremont McKenna College. Indeed, Graglia stated during the seminar that he would permit the Court to overturn an act of Congress or an act of one of the state legislatures only if it was as clearly unconstitutional as would be an act of the Congress or of the state legislatures that provided that women could not vote despite the nineteenth amendment's guarantee of the right to vote on the part of women. See also Speech by Attorney General Edwin Meese III, Federalist Society Lawyers Division (Nov. 15, 1985), reprinted in *The Federalist Society, The Great Debate Interpreting Our Written Constitution* 31, 39 (Occasional Paper No. 2 1986). The power to declare acts of Congress and laws of the states null and void is truly awesome. This power must be used when the Constitution clearly speaks. It should not be used when the Constitution does not.")

86. Statements of both Hamilton and Madison that have been relied on by those supporting judicial review seem to point to a narrow scope for judicial review. For example, Madison referred to judges' being "naturally led to resist every encroachment upon rights expressly stipulated for in the Constitution by the Declaration of Rights." 12 *Papers of James Madison, supra* note 17, at 207. Similarly, Hamilton referred to "all acts contrary to the manifest tenor of the Constitution" as being subject to being declared void by the courts. *The Federalists* No. 78, at 524 (A. Hamilton) (J. Cooke ed. 1961).

87. "The enumeration in the Constitution, of certain rights, shall not be construed to deny of disparage others retained by the people." U.S. Const. amend. IX. The ninth amendment was specifically relied on by Justice Goldberg in his concurring opinion in Griswold v. Connecticut, 381 U.S. 479, 486 (1965) (Goldberg, J., concurring): "The language and history of the Ninth Amendment reveal that the Framers of the Constitution believed that there are additional fundamental rights, protected from governmental infringement, which exist alongside those fundamental rights specifically mentioned in the first eight constitutional amendments." *Id.* at 488. "The Ninth Amendment simply shows the intent of the constitution's authors that other fundamental personal rights should not be denied such protection or disparaged in any other way simply because they are not specifically listed in the first eight constitutional amendments." *Id.* at 492.

Consider also Thomas Grey's evaluation of the ninth amendment:

For the generation that framed the Constitution, the concept of a "higher law," protecting "natural rights," and taking precedence over ordinary positive law as a matter of political obligation, was widely shared and deeply felt. An essential element of American constitutionalism was the reduction to written form – and hence to positive law – of some of the principles of natural rights. But at the same time, it was generally recognized that written constitutions could not completely codify the higher law. Thus in the framing of the original American constitutions it was widely accepted that there remained unwritten but still binding principles of higher law. The ninth amendment is the textual expression of this idea in the federal Constitution. Grey, Do We Have an Unwritten Constitution?, 27 *Stan. L. Rev.* 703, 715-16 (1975).

A similar conclusion was reached by John Kaminski:
> The Founders realized that no statesmen could list every liberty in a bill of rights, so they wrote the Ninth Amendment to affirm the natural rights doctrines of the Declaration of Independence. As a statement that unspecified natural rights exist and are not to be abrogated, the Ninth Amendment stands as a silent sentinel guarding liberties not otherwise named in the Constitution. Kaminski, Restoring the Declaration of Independence – Natural Rights and the Ninth Amendment, in *The Bill of Rights: A Lively Heritage* 150 (J. Kukla ed. 1987).

A somewhat different view was expressed by Russell Caplan, who, in the course of an extensive study of the history of the ninth amendment, concluded, *inter alia*:
> By the provision which ultimately became the ninth amendment, Madison intended to assure the anti-federalists that the Constitution would leave intact those individual rights contained in the state constitutions, statutes, and common law. All of the 'certain rights' enumerated in the Constitution and Bill of Rights were derived from state law, and so the 'others,' that is, 'those rights which were not singled out' for enumeration, were those state laws not selected for inclusion...
>
> ...If natural law is imbedded in the ninth amendment, it is because at the time the ninth was adopted natural law was an integral part of justiciable state law. Caplan, The History and Meaning of the Ninth Amendment, 69 *Va. L. Rev.* 259-60 (1983).

Such a conclusion is consistent with Goldberg's assertion that the framers/ratifiers believed that there are individual rights in addition to those specifically enumerated in the Bill of Rights. The only restrictive aspect of Caplan's conclusions is the possible implication that the rights referred to were specific, well-defined rights apparently tied to state law *at the time of the ratification*. Part of the difficulty with this restrictive notion is illustrated by the Virginia Declaration of Rights, which is itself very general in part:
> That all Men are born equally free and independent, and have certain inherent natural Rights, of which they can not by any Compact, deprive or divest their Posterity; among which are the Enjoyment of Life and Liberty, with the Means of acquiring and possessing Property, and pursuing and obtaining Happiness and Safety. 1 *Mason, supra* note 1, at 277.

And certainly Mason, who occasionally referred to the common law, saw a distinction between the common law and other more general rights, as is demonstrated in his "Objections" to the Constitution:
> There is no Declarations of Rights, and laws of the general government being paramount to the laws and constitutions of the several States, the Declaration of Rights in the separate States are no security. Nor are the people secured even in the enjoyment of the benefit of the common law. 3 *Mason, supra* note 1, at 991.

In this first paragraph of his "Objections" Mason demonstrated quite clearly that, although he was concerned about the absence of protection under the common law, he viewed the common law as distinct from the Declaration of Rights.

Of course, since the Bill of Rights was originally thought to be applicable only to the federal government – see Barron v. Mayor of Baltimore, 32 U.S. (7 Pet.) 243 (1833) – there remains the question of the possible application of the Bill of Rights to the states and the possibility of carrying forward against the states the natural law approach exemplified in the writings of Mason and others.

88. *Cf.* Choper, *supra* note 19 (preferring judicial protection of individual rights, to preserving federalism and separation of powers between the Congress and the President).

89. One may judge from the literature that *Roe v. Wade*, 410 U.S. 113 (1973), in which the Court held that there was a limited right on the part of the woman to have an abortion, is viewed by many as the ultimate instance of judicial activism. Viewed by itself, *Roe* may appear to fit this description. One must remember, however, that by the time the Court decided *Roe v. Wade*, constitutional protection for reproductive freedom had been firmly established. [Although it] would not have been inconsistent with the line of growth of constitutional protection for reproductive freedom for the Court to have held that the asserted governmental interest in protecting potential human life was constitutionally more important than the woman's interest in reproductive freedom[,]...because the court had previously held that reproductive freedom was entitled to constitutional protection, the holding in *Roe*, extending that protection to the abortion decision, was fully consistent with the line of growth of constitutional protection for reproductive freedom. Sedler, The Legitimacy Debate in Constitutional Adjudication, 44 *Ohio St. L.J.*, 119 n.167 (1983).

It must be conceded that acceptance of a broad concept of judicial review does not guarantee the protection of any particular right against state infringement. Although in the last several decades, non-property rights (for example, freedom of speech, equal protection, privacy, and rights of persons accused of crime) have been the focus of attention, there now seems to be a resurgence of interest in the protection of property rights. See generally R. Epstein, *supra* note 7.

90. In an early draft of the Constitution in Philadelphia, Congress was granted the power to "make war." Later, a change was made, as is documented in the following colloquy, as reported by Madison:

Mr. Madison and Mr. Gerry moved to insert 'declare,' striking out 'make' war; leaving to the Executive the power to repel sudden attacks.

Mr. Sharman thought it stood very well. The Executive shd. be able to repel and not to commence war. 'Make' better than 'declare' the latter narrowing the power too much.

Mr. Gerry never expected to hear in a republic a motion to empower the Executive alone to declare war.

Mr. Ellsworth. There is a material difference between the cases of making *war* and making *peace*. It should be more easy to get out of war, than into it. War also is a simple and overt declaration. Peace attended with intricate & secret negotiations.

Mr. Mason was agst. giving the power of war to the Executive, because not safely to be entrusted with it; or to the Senate, because not so constructed as to be entitled to it. He was for clogging rather than facilitating war; but for facilitating peace. He preferred 'declare' to 'make.' On the motion to insert *declare* – in place of make, it was agreed to. *Madison's notes, supra* note 16, at 476.

91. In light of the difficulty of looking to the past for the resolution of contemporary constitutional problems – indeed, in light of disagreements over whether and the extent to which one should even try to look to the past (see generally Brest, *supra* note 75) – the reader may legitimately inquire whether I have anything positive

to offer. My answer is that I have offered a solution, albeit a procedural one: I have advocated selection of judges by lot from a large list of candidates selected by a broadly representative commission; I have done so for the same reason that we select six to twelve jurors to decide a case – namely, that there is no better way to do it. In the absence of consensus about how to interpret the Constitution, for example, we ought to assure that judges as a whole are broadly representative of the community attitudes towards this subject. Davidow, Judicial Selection: The Search for Quality and Representativeness, 31 *Case W. Res. L. Rev.* 409 (1981). My procedural solution is thus a more mechanical one than the procedural one offered by John Hart Ely. See J. Ely, *Democracy and Distrust* 181 (1980)("elaboration of a representation-reinforcing theory of judicial review" without regard to the "substantive merits of the political choice under attack").

GEORGE MASON AND THE LEGACY OF CONSTITUTIONAL LIBERTY

An Examination of the Influence of George Mason on the American Bill of Rights

Section 3: The Lasting Influence

"George Mason — His Lasting Influence"
by Sandra Day O'Connor

"George Mason: Influence Beyond the United States"
by Edward W. Chester

"George Mason: Why the Forgotten Founding Father"
by Donald J. Senese

GEORGE MASON – HIS LASTING INFLUENCE

by Sandra Day O'Connor

The bicentennial of our Constitution which we celebrate this year is an occasion to look back at the origins of the document that created our national government.

Two hundred years ago this past summer, 55 delegates from 12 of the 13 states then in existence met in Philadelphia in what we called at the time "The Grand Convention." Thirty-three of the delegates were lawyers or had studied law. The Virginia delegation to the Convention was selected early, and its composition was so impressive that other states were stimulated to follow suit. The Virginia delegation, as all of you students of history know, was headed by George Washington, and included James Madison, George Wythe and John Blair of Williamsburg, Governor Edmund Randolph, Dr. James McClurg of Richmond, and, of course, George Mason, the squire of Gunston Hall. A more impressive delegation could not be found, and this group of Virginians first developed and presented the framework of our Constitution. Their efforts, including those of George Mason, who ultimately opposed ratification of the Constitution, provided much of the substance of the new Constitution.

Mason was influential and highly respected in the public affairs of Virginia. As author of the Fairfax County Resolves of 1774 and Virginia's Declaration of Rights in 1776, he was already experienced in drafting public statements of principles. Although he preferred his private life, he agreed to attend the conference on the navigation of the Potomac at Mt. Vernon in 1785. He was elected to the Virginia Legislature, and was chosen to be a delegate at the Annapolis Convention in 1786, an appointment which he refused on account of illness. To the surprise of many, he accepted his selection as a delegate to the Philadelphia Convention. He set out for that city in the summer of 1787 at age 62 on the longest journey of his life. Having experienced a few weeks at the Convention, he soon wrote his family that he "would not, upon pecuniary motives, serve in this convention for a thousand pounds per day." But serve he did, without pay, from the first day on May 29 to the last on September 17, working faithfully and industriously and apprehensively, to the end, hoping to achieve his goals. Each of his proposals was rejected: a bill of rights, an end to the importation of slaves, and a requirement of a 2/3 majority vote in Congress for Navigation Acts.

When the Convention finally voted on the Constitution as a whole on the afternoon of September 15, there were 3 delegates who could not overcome their doubts about the wisdom of the summer's work — Governor Randolph, Elbridge Gerry and George Mason. Randolph moved that the draft Constitution be referred to state conventions for suggested amendments, which would then be submitted to another general convention. George Mason seconded the motion and agreed with Randolph on the dangerous power and structure of the proposed new government. Mason concluded that "it would end either in monarchy or a tyrannical aristocracy; which, he was in doubt, but one or the other, he was sure." Madison's notes record Mason as saying, "As the Constitution now stands I could neither give it my support or vote in Virginia; and I could not sign here what I could not support there."

Randolph's motion failed. The delegates would not agree to another convention. The final draft of the Constitution was printed and the original engrossed on parchment. The delegates reassembled for the last time on Monday, September 17, to listen to Dr. Franklin's often quoted speech, to make one last change, and then to sign "the unanimous consent of the states" — all, that is, except Randolph, Gerry and Mason.

The anti-federalists argued the case against ratification eloquently and passionately. Virginia's state convention did not assemble until June, 1788, by which time 8 states had voted for ratification. A 9th state's ratification would seal the union. Governor Randolph repented and supported the Federalists, urging ratification. George Mason, Patrick Henry, James Monroe and William Grayson led the debate against ratification. The Virginia debates were the best reported of any convention — and among the longest, lasting 4 weeks. On June 25 the Virginia Convention voted to ratify by 89 to 79, and included recommendations for a bill of rights.

George Mason lost his battle against ratification, but his ideals and political activities have significantly influenced our constitutional jurisprudence. He has contributed in three ways: his participation at the Constitutional Convention helped to shape the final product; his speeches in opposition to ratification provided insight into the contemporary understanding of how the new government would operate; and, most importantly, his work on the Virginia Declaration of Rights served as the model for our Bill of Rights and has helped define those rights.

Many weeks of the Convention at Philadelphia were spent on the question of how the legislature should be constituted. The smaller states advocated giving each State an equal vote, while the larger states favored representation that was proportional to population. George Mason was among the latter. Madison's notes reflect that Mason "argued strongly for an election of the larger branch by the people. It was to be the grand depository of the democratic principle of the Govt." The Great Compromise resolved the deadlock by providing for equal representation of States in the Senate, and representation proportional to population in the House. Mason served on the Committee of Eleven which recommended the compromise. The Supreme Court recounted this history in *Wesberry* v. *Sanders*, 376 U. S. 1, a case decided in 1964. On this basis, the Court concluded that "as nearly as is practicable one man's vote in a congressional election is to be worth as much as another's." The Court consequently invalidated Georgia's apportionment statute because it created congressional districts having vastly different numbers of voters.

Mason also spoke often at the Convention against slavery. He objected to the second significant compromise, which forbade Congress to interfere with the slave trade until 1808, and struck out the requirement of a 2/3 vote for navigation acts.

He was instrumental in lowering the vote needed to override a Presidential veto from 3/4 to 2/3 of both Houses of Congress. And he was the first to ask specifically that a Bill of Rights be included in the new Charter.

George Mason's remarks at the ratification debates have been cited by the Supreme Court over a span of 100 years as the Supreme Court has wrestled with the problem of interpreting the Eleventh Amendment. The Eleventh Amendment explicitly forbids suits in federal court by a citizen against a State other than his own. In *Hans* v. *Louisiana*, 134 U. S. 1, a case decided in 1890, the Supreme Court ruled that individuals may not sue their own State governments, either, without the state's consent. The Court relied on the concept of State sovereign immunity. The Court noted that at the Virginia Convention, George Mason had objected to the proposed Constitution on the ground that it permitted citizens to sue their own State governments. Madison and Marshall had argued that federal courts would hear such cases only if the State itself brought the suit, or if the State consented to be sued. The Supreme Court adopted the view of Madison and Marshall as the correct interpretation of the Constitution. In successive cases, the Court had ruled that citizens may not sue their own States under federal law in federal court without the State's consent.

Recently, in dissent, Justice Brennan has taken the position that Mason's fears concerning abrogation of state sovereign immunity were better founded than Marshall and Madison were willing to admit. Justice Brennan has referred to Mason's views in urging the Court to reverse the *Hans* v. *Louisiana* case.

George Mason's greatest contribution to present day Constitutional law was his influence on our Bill of Rights — the first 10 Amendments to our Constitution. Mason drafted the Virginia Declaration of Rights in 1776, soon after the State of Virginia became independent. The document inspired similar declarations in other States. It also became the model for the Bill of Rights. The Supreme Court has cited Mason frequently when interpreting the first ten Amendments. The historical background is particularly important in interpreting the religion clauses of the First Amendment.

The First Amendment provides that "Congress shall make no law respecting an establishment of religion, or prohibiting the free exercise thereof." The origin of this clause is Mason's first draft of the Virginia Declaration of Rights. Mason's version said:

"That as Religion, or the Duty which we owe to our divine and omnipotent Creator, and the Manner of discharging it, can be governed only by Reason and Conviction, not by Force or Violence; and therefore that all Men shou'd enjoy the fullest Toleration in the Exercise of Religion, according to the Dictates of Conscience, unpunished and unrestrained by the Magistrate, unless, under Colour of Religion, any Man disturb the Peace, the Happiness, or Safety of Society, or of Individuals. And that it is the mutual Duty of all, to practice Christian Forbearance, Love and Charity towards Each other."

This formulation is entirely consistent with Mason's quiet and retiring habits, and his affection for leading a private life at Gunston Hall. James Madison modified Mason's draft before it was enacted as the Virginia Declaration of Rights, putting it in language more familiar to our ears today. But the development of the notion of separation of church and state did not end there. Eight years later, Virginia enacted Thomas Jefferson's Bill Against Religious Assessments, which had Mason's enthusiastic support. This law first introduced the idea that the government should not contribute financially to the establishment of any religion.

The development of the separation of church and state in Virginia has influenced the Supreme Court's interpretation of the religion clauses of the First Amendment. Justice Powell wrote an opinion referring to this history. The case was *Edwards* v. *Aguillard*, 107 S. Ct. 2573, in which the Court struck down a Louisiana law that required creation science to be taught whenever evolution science was taught. Justice Powell's concurring opinion agreed that the Louisiana law was unconstitutional. However, Justice Powell also explained that the First Amendment does not categorically prohibit discussing religion in the classroom. For example, he observed that it would be entirely appropriate to study the religious beliefs of George Mason and the other Founding Fathers and how those beliefs influenced the Constitution. As Justice Powell noted, one must study the context in which the First Amendment developed in order to understand it correctly.

The Supreme Court has observed that the history of the separation of church and state in Virginia is one of progress towards a more clearly marked division between church and state: from toleration, to free exercise, to disestablishment. The Supreme Court first noted this progression, and George Mason's role in it, in *Everson* v. *Board of Education*, 330 U. S. 1. The Court decided *Everson* in 1947. The majority upheld a New Jersey statute that reimbursed parents for the cost of transporting their children by public transportation to private sectarian schools. Justice Rutledge dissented and explained how in his view even this relationship between church and state would have been offensive to the Virginians who developed the First Amendment.

Justice Rutledge's dissenting opinion in *Everson* later was cited with approval in the Supreme Court's decision in *Committee for Public Education* v. *Nyquist*, 413 U. S. 756, a case decided in 1973. *Nyquist* invalidated a New York statute that provided several types of aid to private sectarian schools, including provisions for repairs to schools, reimbursement of lower-income families for tuition, and tax subsides to other families. The majority opinion in *Nyquist* concluded that all these provisions violated the First Amendment's prohibition against an establishment of religion. The Court's opinion explicitly refers to George Mason's contribution to this doctrine.

The Supreme Court has also referred to Mason when interpreting the free speech guaranty of the First Amendment. In *Joseph Burstyn, Inc.* v. *Wilson*, 343 U. S. 495, a case decided in 1952, the Court struck down a New York law that prohibited showing "sacrilegious" films. The film in question, *The Miracle*, told the story of a demented shepherdess who believed that St. Joseph was responsible for the birth of her illegitimate son. Justice Frankfurter wrote a concurring opinion that agreed that the New York statute was invalid. However, Justice Frankfurter also advocated interpreting the free speech clause moderately and reasonably, as he thought Mason himself would have done. Justice Frankfurter stated:

> "It would startle Madison and Jefferson and George Mason, could they adjust themselves to our day, to be told that the freedom of speech which they espoused in the Bill of Rights authorizes a showing of "*The Miracle*" from windows facing St. Patrick's Cathedral in the forenoon of Easter Sunday, just as it would startle them to be told that any picture, whatever its theme and its expression, could be barred from being commercially exhibited. The general principle of free speech, expressed in the First Amendment as to encroachments by Congress, and included as it is in the Fourteenth Amendment, binding on the States, must be placed in its historical and legal contexts."

George Mason's writings also have been particularly important to the Supreme Court when it considers which rights in the Bill of Rights are so fundamental that they restrain State governments as well as the National government. As enacted, of course, the Bill of Rights limited only what the National government could do. It did not apply to the States. Parts of the Bill of Rights, however, have been applied to the States through the Fourteenth Amendment. The Fourteenth Amendment says that "No State shall... deprive any person of life, liberty or property, without due process of law." If a right listed in the Bill of Rights is fundamental, the Supreme Court will construe it as part of due process of law and prevent State governments from interfering with it. The Supreme Court often relies on history in order to determine which rights are fundamental. George Mason is important in this context. Mason drafted the Virginia Declaration of Rights in accordance with the traditional rights of Englishmen. Those traditional rights are more likely to be part of fundamental due process than privileges of more recent vintage.

For example, the Supreme Court quoted Mason when it determined that the Sixth Amendment's guarantee of a speedy trial in criminal prosecutions is so fundamental that State governments may not infringe it. The case was *Klopfer v. North Carolina*, 386 U. S. 213, decided in 1967. The North Carolina law permitted a prosecutor to postpone a prosecution indefinitely, as long as the suspect was not imprisoned. In its opinion, the Supreme Court noted that the Magna Carta had guaranteed prompt trial. Sir Edward Coke had confirmed that this was a fundamental put of the law of England. Thus it was "not surprising" that George Mason included the guarantee of a speedy trial in the Virginia Declaration of Rights. The ancient origins of the right to a speedy trial indicate that it is a fundamental right protected by the due process clause of the Fourteenth Amendment. Accordingly, the Supreme Court invalidated the North Carolina law.

Lest you think we always have agreed with Mr. Mason, I should note that his views have not always carried the day. In *Twining v. New Jersey*, 211 U. S. 78, a case decided in 1908, the Supreme Court held that the First Amendment's privilege against self-incrimination is not a fundamental right protected by the due process clause of the Fourteenth

Amendment. Justice Harlan dissented in that case relying on the views of George Mason. Justice Harlan related how:

> "Virginia, in its Convention of May, 1776... made a Declaration (drawn entirely by the celebrated George Mason) which set forth certain rights as pertaining to the people of that State and to their posterity "as the basis and foundation of government." Among those rights (that famous Declaration distinctly announced) was the right of a person not to be compelled to give evidence against himself..... [W]hen the first Congress met, there was entire unanimity among statesmen of that day as to the necessity and wisdom of having a National Bill of Rights which would, beyond all question, secure against Federal encroachment all the rights, privileges and immunities which, everywhere and by everybody in America, were then recognized as fundamental in Anglo-American liberty...."

Despite Justice Harlan's argument that Mason and the Framers viewed the privilege against self incrimination as fundamental, the majority in *Twining* did not deem it to be incorporated by the due process clause of the Fourteenth Amendment. In the end, however, Justice Harlan and George Mason were vindicated. In 1964, the Supreme Court expressly overruled *Twining* in the case of *Malloy* v. *Hogan*, 378 U.S. 1. In language which Mason would have applauded, the Court held that the privilege against self incrimination *is* one of the fundamental rights protected by the due process clause of the Fourteenth Amendment against State as well as Federal interference.

The Supreme Court also quoted George Mason in a case in which it decided that the Eighth Amendment's prohibition against "cruel and unusual punishments" extended to punishments disproportionate to the crime. In *Solem* v. *Helm*, 463 U. S. 277, decided in 1983, the Court studied the history of the Eighth Amendment to decide whether it forbade disproportionate as well as barbaric punishments. The Court discerned a principle of proportional punishment in English law. It traced this principle from the English Bill of Rights through Mason's Declaration of Rights to its present form in the Bill of Rights. The Court quoted George Mason explaining, "We claim Nothing but the Liberties & Privileges of Englishmen, in the same Degree, as if we had still continued along our Brethren in Great Britain... We have received [these rights] from our Ancestors, and, with God's Leave, we will transmit them, unimpaired to our Posterity." This articulation of the historical link between the Eighth Amendment and the rights of Englishmen enabled the Supreme Court to conclude that disproportionate punishments were prohibited by the Eighth and Fourteenth Amendments to the Constitution.

It was not until the adoption of the post Civil War amendments to the Constitution that this nation finally abolished slavery and rejected its lingering effects. But George Mason opposed slavery from the very start. At the convention, George Mason strongly supported a ban on the importation of slaves — a first step toward the abolition of slavery.

My purpose has been to describe how George Mason's work and thought has affected decisions by the Court on which I sit, and, thus, the application of our Constitution to modern life. As an author of the Virginia Declaration of Rights, as a drafter at the Constitutional Convention, and as a participant in the ratification debates, George Mason has influenced significantly the way in which we interpret the Constitution today. His refusal to sign the Constitution has not prevented him from being one of its authors in an important sense. During the Constitutional Convention, Mason said it "could not be expected to make a faultless Government," and that he would "prefer trusting to posterity the amendment of its defects, rather than push the experiment too far." Perhaps you will agree with me that, if George Mason were with us today, he would agree that posterity has been worthy of his trust through our contemporary application of some of his most cherished concepts as provided in the Bill of Rights and in the 14th Amendment.

GEORGE MASON: INFLUENCE BEYOND THE UNITED STATES

by Dr. Edward W. Chester

One speaks of the "facts" of history; the names, the places, the dates, the events which make up the historical narrative. About these scholars are usually (but not always) in agreement. We know, for example, that George Mason was born in Virginia in 1725 and died there in 1792. On the other hand, historical causation is a much more complex phenomenon. What caused the American Revolution? What caused the French Revolution? Obviously there were a number of factors impacting on each event. An even more difficult task for the historian is to ascertain the degree to which the leading thinkers in America, England, and France influenced each other during the Eighteenth Century. A case in point is the relationship between the Virginia Declaration of Rights of 1776 drawn up by George Mason, the American Declaration of Independence written by Thomas Jefferson three weeks later, and the French Declaration of the Rights of Man and the Citizen of 1789.

Quite often historians recognize the accomplishments of an individual in their writings. Thomas Jefferson, Benjamin Franklin, and Thomas Paine are cases in point from the era of the American Revolution. Then there are those individuals whose achievements are either underrated or overlooked. George Mason is an outstanding example from the same period of United States history.

Although Mason's Virginia Declaration of Rights antedated Jefferson's American Declaration of Independence, scholars all too often have portrayed Thomas Jefferson as the sole author of the latter document. Unquestionably one of the most shameful examples of neglect which one might cite is Carl Becker's classic 1922 work *The Declaration of*

Independence: A Study in the History of Political Ideas. According to the index, there is not a single reference to George Mason in his book. Towards the close of his narrative Becker writes that: "In 1783, Lafayette conspicuously placed a copy of the Declaration (of Independence) in his house, leaving beside it a vacant space to be filled, as we are told, by a declaration of rights for France when, if ever, France should have one."[1] Thus Thomas Jefferson here is given full credit for influencing the 1789 French document, George Mason none at all.

Equally interesting is the failure of the author to mention George Mason in such well-known surveys of Franco-American relations as Lewis Rosenthal, *America and France* (1882) and Beckles Willson, *America's Ambassadors to France* (1928). Rosenthal and Willson instead focus their attention on such American liberals physically present in France at one time or another as Thomas Jefferson, Benjamin Franklin, and Thomas Paine, as well as on such visiting conservatives as John Adams and Gouverneur Morris whose enthusiasm for the French Revolution was minimal at best. They ignore the fact that a thinker's ideas may cross the Atlantic Ocean without the individual himself or herself making the trans-Atlantic voyage. Unlike many of his colleagues, George Mason basically lived out his life in his native Virginia, with Gunston Hall near Mount Vernon as his headquarters.

More recently, however, historians have begun to give Mason his just due, in accordance with the opinion of the late Eighteenth Century French mathematician and philosopher the Marquis de Condorcet. Condorcet stated in his *Ideas on Despotism* that the Virginian had authored the first systematic declaration of the rights of man, and therefore had earned the eternal gratitude of mankind. Therefore, it is highly appropriate that the modern American scholar R. R. Palmer in his *The Age of the Democratic Revolution: A Political History of Europe and America, 1760-1800* (1959) includes as his fourth appendix (pp. 518-21) excerpts from the Virginia Declaration of Rights, alongside their counterparts from the French Declaration of the Rights of Man and the Citizen. In his commentary Palmer observes that:[2]

There was in fact a remarkable parallelism between the French Declaration and the Virginia Declaration of 1776. The parallelism can readily be explained by the presence of Jefferson in Paris and the activity of his friend Lafayette in the preparation of the French document; but this explanation is hardly necessary, since the wording of the first three articles, the principal articles of the French Declaration, was devised not by Lafayette but by Mounier, who, though, familiar with American bills of rights, was not in much contact with Jefferson."

As Thomas Jefferson spent a number of years in France, Lafayette also spent a number of years in America during the Revolutionary War era. While he was here Lafayette not only fought at the Battle of Brandywine and at Monmouth, but also acquainted himself with the ideology and philosophy underlying the American cause. Thus he became familiar with both Jefferson's American Declaration of Independence and Mason's Virginia Declaration of Rights. If not the sole author of the French Declaration of the Rights of Man and the Citizen in 1789, as a member of the National Assembly Lafayette played an important role in the shaping of that document.

Another prominent American scholar, many of whose writings focus on the colonial period, is Richard Morris. Morris also has recognized that the French drew upon Mason as much as upon Jefferson in writing their revolutionary proclamation in 1789. He strongly makes this point in his thought-provoking monograph *The Emerging Nations and the American Revolution* (1970). Pointing out that there were constant references to seminal American political documents in the course of the debate in the French National Assembly, Morris observes that:[3]

"The Virginia statesman George Mason might well have instituted an action of plagiarism against the author of the Declaration of the Rights of Man and the Citizen which the French National Assembly adopted on August 26, 1789. The resemblance to Mason's Bill of Rights which the Virginia Assembly had enacted back in June of 1776 is too close to be coincidental. Even the sequence in which the ideas are presented is almost identical. Both affirm the equality of man, the security of all men's rights to life, liberty, and property, and the doctrine of popular sovereignty."

What is so interesting about this seemingly effortless transfer of political ideas from one nation to another is that the situation in America in 1776 was quite different from that in France during 1789. America was then a colony of England, while France was an independent nation. After obtaining its independence the United States opted for a President rather than a King, while a decade after the execution of King Louis XVI of France Napoleon proclaimed himself the Emperor of his people. Despite what seemed to many Britishers and continental Europeans at the time as a rather "radical" revolution, moreover, there was no large-scale social upheaval in the United States as there was in France, where both the nobility and the clergy played an important political role. Americans who remained loyal to the mother country during the Revolutionary period did in many cases experience social ostracism and eventual self-exile, but rarely, if ever, death, while the French guillotine wrote *finis* to the lives of many of the victims of the Revolution, the Jacobin leader Robespierre as well as King Louis XVI.

Since France had helped America win its independence from England, not only through the presence of Lafayette in this country, but also thanks to the Franco-American Alliance of 1778, it is not surprising that there was a widespread feeling of gratitude towards that nation throughout the United States between that date and the outbreak of the French Revolution in 1789. Nevertheless, there also were a large number of Anglophiles, including such Federalist leaders as John Adams and Alexander

Hamilton. Basically conservative men, these individuals came to look with displeasure on the French Revolution. In contrast, more liberal-minded individuals such as Benjamin Franklin, Thomas Paine, Thomas Jefferson, and George Mason were more sympathetic towards the moderate phases of that great upheaval which displaced the old regime from power in France. Thus it is only appropriate that it was such an individual as Mason who influenced the 1789 French Declaration of the Rights of Man and the Citizen rather than one of his more conservative American colleagues.

It obviously is impossible properly to compare Mason's Virginia Declaration of Rights of 1776 with its trans-Atlantic counterpart of 13 years later without quoting key passages from each document. There follows the introduction and the first three paragraphs in Mason's own words:[4]

> "A Declaration of Rights made by the Representatives of the good people of Virginia, assembled in full and free Convention; which rights do pertain to them and their posterity, as the basis and foundation of Government.
>
> 1) That all men are by nature equally free and independent, and have certain inherent rights, of which when they enter into a state of society, they cannot, by any compact, deprive or divest their posterity; namely, the enjoyment of life and liberty, with the means of acquiring and possessing property, and pursuing and obtaining happiness and safety.
> 2) That all power is vested in, and consequently derived from the People; the magistrates are their trustees and servants, and at all times amenable to them.
> 3) That Government is, or ought to be, instituted for the common benefit, protection, and security of the people, nation, or community; of all the various modes and forms of Government that is best which is capable of producing the greatest degree of happiness and

safety, and is most effectually secured against the danger of mal-administration; and that, whenever any Government shall be found inadequate or contrary to these purposes, a majority of the community hath an indubitable, inalienable, and indefeasible right, to reform, alter, or abolish it, in such manner as shall be judged most conducive to the publick weal."

The similarities between these excerpts from George Mason's Virginia Declaration of Rights and certain passages in Thomas Jefferson's subsequent American Declaration of Independence are so obvious that one is hardly able to ignore them. Why, then, is it that many scholars have regarded Jefferson's trans-Atlantic influence as greater? There are several reasons for this. First of all, Jefferson's Declaration was for all thirteen Atlantic Coast colonies, Mason's for a single state (Virginia). Secondly, in the opinion of this author, Jefferson was probably a more gifted literary stylist than Mason, capable of more memorable phrasing. A third reason is the fact that Jefferson was actually present in France at the beginning of the Revolution there, while Mason remained at home in Virginia.

How is it, then, that the more provincial Mason was just as capable of lofty political thinking as was Jefferson? Much has been made of the size of the latter's library at Monticello. Mason, though, spent much of his youth with his guardian uncle, John Mercer, who himself possessed a rather considerable library of 1,500 volumes. Here the young Mason read such works as Montaigne's *Essays*, Raleigh's *History of the World*, Hawkin's *Crown Law*, Salmon's *History of England*, and Locke's *Works*. Although he himself never was a lawyer, Mason was quite familiar with such important constitutional documents from Great Britain as the *Magna Carta*, the Petition of Right, and the Bill of Rights. He also was exposed to the leading writers of the ancient world (Homer, Virgil, Ovid, Plutarch, Juvenal, Horace, Marcus Aurelius, Plato, and Seneca), as well as a number of their modern counterparts (Dante, Tasso, Milton, Pope, Dryden, and Shakespeare.)

Therefore in the case of Mason one should not conclude from his relative geographical immobility that he was guilty of a corresponding intellectual stagnation.

If Mason merely copied what others before him wrote, why, then, bother to study him? That Mason did not merely paraphrase the key documents of British constitutional liberty, but instead went beyond them, is shown by Lyon G. Tyler, who observes with respect to the Bill of Rights that:[5]

> "It was from the pen of the celebrated lawyer Somers, but it does not approach the instrument written in the quiet of Gunston Hall. Somers, having little or no thought of popular government — a conception which was to await the American example — left the prerogatives of the Crown unimpaired, and the authority of Parliament beyond any definite control by the people. Even so, the liberal spirit evidenced in the work of Somers and other Whig leaders marked the slow dawn of a new day for Englishmen."

Armistead Churchill, in an unpublished study of *George Mason and the Bill of Rights,* similarly points out that in his thinking the Virginian went beyond the two leading Seventeenth Century British constitutional documents. He writes:[6]

> "The design, the conciseness, the unity and thought (of the 1776 Virginia Declaration) were peculiarly those of its author. The English Petition of Right addressed to Charles I was only an enumeration of the laws that had been violated, and a prayer that they might be preserved. The English Declaration of Rights on the accession of William and Mary was 'wholly historical and retrospective in its scope.' Neither of these great monuments of English liberty was, like the Virginia Bill of Rights, of universal application everywhere and for all time."

As for perhaps the greatest British spokesman for individual rights during the Seventeenth Century, John Locke, he stressed life, liberty, and property, in his *Treatise on Civil Government*. So did George Mason, but Mason added happiness and safety to his basic list in the Virginia Declaration of Rights. Shortly thereafter, when Thomas Jefferson wrote the American Declaration of Independence, he emphasized life, liberty, and the pursuit of happiness. Jefferson, however, omitted property. He apparently had been influenced by the Scottish Enlightenment leader Francis Hutcheson, whose moral and political philosophy made happiness a prime virtue. As for the French Declaration of the Rights of Man and the Citizen, its list of basic Rights is slightly different: liberty, property, security and resistance to oppression.

Within the span of three months two momentous events occurred, one on each side of the Atlantic Ocean. On April 30, 1789 George Washington was sworn in as the first President of the United States. This established a precedent of two centuries of uninterrupted Presidential rule in the United States, accompanied by quadrennial elections and the peaceful transfer of political power from one administration to another. On the other hand, on July 14, 1789 an angry French mob stormed the Bastille prison, triggering a revolution which was to have far-reaching implications equal to those of its American predecessor of 1776. Taking as their slogan "Liberty, Equality, and Fraternity," the French revolutionaries ushered in a new era of European history.

Like the American Declaration of Independence, the French Declaration of the Rights of Man and the Citizen was drawn up at the very beginning of the revolutionary period, approximately six weeks after the fall of the Bastille. Appropriately it was Lafayette — an honorary citizen of Virginia — who proposed that the National Assembly adopt some type of political catechism. Lafayette also presented to that body the various bills and declarations of rights approved by the American states, including that which George Mason had drawn up for Virginia in 1776. The French National Assembly took the position that it was fitting that France should look to America for advice, since the former had helped the latter win its liberty, and now the United States was demonstrating how a nation should preserve its liberties.

There follow the two introductory paragraphs and the first three articles of the French Declaration of the Rights of Man and the Citizen:[7]

> "The representatives of the French people, organized in National Assembly, considering that ignorance, forgetfulness, or contempt of the rights of man are the sole cause of public misfortune and of the corruption of government, have resolved to set forth in a solemn declaration the natural, inalienable, and sacred rights of man, in order that such declaration, continually before all members of the social body, may be a perpetual reminder of their rights and duties; in order that the acts of the legislative power and those of the executive power may constantly be compared with the aim of every political institution and may accordingly be more respected; in order that the demands of the citizens, founded henceforth upon simple and incontestable principles, may always be directed towards the maintenance of the Constitution and the welfare of all.
>
> Accordingly, the National Assembly recognizes and proclaims, in the presence and under the auspices of the Supreme Being, the following rights of man and citizen.
>
> 1. Men are born and remain free and equal in rights; sound distinctions may be based only upon general usefulness.
>
> 2. The aim of every political association is the preservation of the natural and inalienable rights of man; these rights are liberty, property, security, and resistance to oppression.
>
> 3. The source of all sovereignty resided essential-

ly in the nation; no group, no individual may exercise authority not emanating expressly therefrom."

Elsewhere the French Declaration of the Rights of Man copies a number of the ideas set forth in George Mason's Virginia Declaration of Rights, yet the order in which these appear is not the same. Among these ideas are the separation of powers, the right to vote, fair trials, no inhumane punishments, restrictions on the police, freedom of the press, and freedom of religion. While Mason included fourteen articles, moreover, the French expanded the number to seventeen.

This French Declaration of the Rights of Man and the Citizen, despite its revolutionary tone, still in many ways is bourgeois in character. It fails to place an adequate emphasis on economic principles, and it does not precisely define what constitutes private property. In addition, it places an inadequate emphasis on the right of association. Nor were all of its principles eventually included in the French Constitution.

As for the differences between George Mason's Virginia Declaration of Rights and its French counterpart, one of the most perceptive extended analyses of both documents is that of R. R. Palmer:[8]

"The Virginia declaration differs from the French in its emphasis on freedom and frequency of elections and on jury trial, in its concrete warnings against excessive bail, general warrants, suspending of laws and standing armies, and its more explicit reference to Christian and moral virtues. The French declaration differs from that of Virginia in its clearer formulation of citizenship, its definition of law as the expression of the general will, its definition of liberty as the right to do what does not harm another, its more explicit provision that the law must be the same for all and public office open to all alike on the basis of abilities, its greater reserve in relating freedom of thought and religion to law and order, its provision that property may be taken for public use only with due compensation, its less explicit reference to moral virtues and its adoption of a deistic rather than a Christian tone."

How did George Mason react to the swiftly unfolding series of events in France during the remaining three years of his life? The mere fact that the National Assembly copied his Virginia Declaration of Rights does not mean that he uncritically accepted the various aspects of the French Revolution *in toto*. That he had certain reservations about developments across the Atlantic is attested to by the comments which he made in certain letters during this period, some of them to his son John, who spent considerable time in the French city of Bordeaux.

On September 8, 1789 George Mason wrote Samuel Griffin from Gunston Hall that "These people seem to have catched the Flame of American Freedom; and in protecting the Rights & Liberty of others, have learned to assert their own.[9] But by the following Spring doubts had begun to undermine Mason's earlier optimistic assessment of developments in France. This is revealed in a letter which he wrote to John Mason from Gunston Hall on May 20, 1790:[10]

> "I heartily wish the French Nation Success in establishing their new Government, upon the Principles of Liberty, & the sacred Rights of human Nature; but I dread the Consequences of their Affairs remaining so long in an unsettled State. Their Finances, their Commerce, & some of their most important Interests, must suffer exceedingly by it; besides the Risque of the most respectable Part of the People (which is always found in the Middle Walks of Life) being disgusted, and worn down, with so long a Scene of Doubt & Uncertainty, not to say Anarchy."

Mason later was reassured about the state of French finances, as he confided to Thomas Jefferson (now Secretary of State) in a letter from Gunston Hall dated January 10, 1791. Mason began by observing that: "As I well know your Attachment to the sacred Cause of Liberty must interest you in the Success of the French Revolution, it is with great Pleasure I can inform you, that it is still going on prosperously; notwithstanding the Evils which have been predicted from the large Emissions of Paper Money."[11] The proceeds from the sale of church and crown lands apparently were more than covering the issue of this paper currency. Three months later, in reflecting on developments across the Atlantic, George Mason wrote his son John from Gunston Hall on April 16 that: "...the French Revolution, from the Beginning has been attended with such extraordinary Circumstances, that the Man who judges of it, by Comparison with anything else, in the Annals of Mankind, will probably find himself mistaken."[12]

On October 7, 1792 George Mason died. He thus was spared learning of the execution of King Louis XVI of France on January 21, 1793, and the establishment of the Reign of Terror conducted under the auspices of the Committee of Public Safety between April 1793 and July 1794. On February 1, 1793 France declared war on England and the Netherlands, but the United States, rather than assist its Revolutionary War ally, instead endorsed a Proclamation of Neutrality. One only is able to wonder as to how George Mason would have reacted to these events.

The influence of George Mason on the French Declaration of Rights of Man and the Citizen should be clear to the reader by now. But Mason also may have had an impact on British history as well, specifically with respect to the abolition of slavery throughout the British Empire in 1833. Antislavery agitation had already begun in the United States by the time of its independence, thanks to the efforts of the Quakers and others, but George Mason also played a significant role in this crusade. He gave one of the greatest speeches of his life at the Constitutional Convention of 1787 in opposition to the nefarious trans-Atlantic traffic. Mason was one of the three delegates at this gathering who refused to sign the complete document, which failed to include a bill of rights.

In this Philadelphia address — which apparently displeased George Washington — Mason observed:[13]

> "Look at your North, then at your South. Where are Southern skills, Southern manufacturing? Slavery discourages arts and manufactures. Where is the poor, hard-working farmer? The poor despise labor, because it is performed by slaves. Slaves prevent the immigration of white settlers who really enrich and strengthen a country.
>
> Keeping slaves produces the most pernicious effect on manners. Every master of slaves is born a petty tyrant. Slaves bring the judgment of Heaven upon a country. As nations cannot be rewarded or punished in the next world, they must be punished in this world....by an inevitable chain of cause and effects, providence punishes national sins by national calamities."

By this time, however, the delegates to the Constitutional Convention had decided not to interfere with the right of any state to import slaves for the next twenty years. Finally, on January 1, 1808 the Constitutional prohibition on the trans-Atlantic slave trade went into effect, Nevertheless, the illegal importation of blacks into the United States did continue on a limited scale up to the outbreak of the Civil War.

As for the nations of Europe, Denmark forbade its citizens to engage in the slave trade as early as 1805, with the British following suit in 1807 and the Dutch in 1814. Then in 1833 Great Britain abolished slavery throughout its empire, with the government paying 20 million pounds sterling to the slaveowners in compensation. Ironically, slavery itself remained legal until 1865 in the United States, which along with Brazil and Cuba was one of the last three nations in the world to abolish the peculiar institution.

Historians generally assign much of the credit for the abolition of slavery throughout the British Empire to William Wilberforce. Nevertheless, opposition to the peculiar institution was unquestionably one of the most consistent features of George Mason's public career, despite the fact that he was a Southerner. In the Virginian's own words, "Such a trade is diabolical in itself and disgraceful to mankind."[14] As a matter of fact, Mason's proposals for the abolition of slavery in the United States were closely parallel to those which the British Parliament adopted in 1833. Mason was of the opinion that slaves should receive an education before they were freed, and that the property rights of the slave owner should also be recognized.

France and England were by no means the only European countries where the influence of Mason's Virginia Declaration of Rights was evident. In 1814 Norway abandoned its union with Denmark and held a constitutional assembly, whose members studied a French translation of American state constitutions (including that of Virginia) with their bills of rights. Seven years later, at the time that Greece revolted against Turkey, the Greek Assembly praised the United States for first proclaiming "those rights to which all men are by nature entitled." Then in 1848 revolutionary agitation shook a number of European nations. The short-lived Frankfurt Assembly in what is now Germany borrowed those provisions from the American Bill of Rights (which were not a part of the original Constitution) guaranteeing the fundamental rights of its citizens against intrusion by member states. Finally, one might cite the successful Italian unification movement, which in the years prior to 1870 also modelled itself partly on the American example. But reform did not uniformly sweep Europe between 1789 and 1900. Such nations as Russia, Austria-Hungary, and Turkey maintained their generally conservative, even reactionary, policies during these years, despite the fact that elsewhere on the continent the winds of change were blowing.

Throughout the Nineteenth Century the American tradition of liberty as espoused by George Mason in his

Virginia Declaration of Rights also exerted an influence elsewhere in the world. As for Latin America and its wars of liberation against Spain, the United States officially recognized the new republics, then proclaimed the separate status of the Old World and the New in the Monroe Doctrine. Following independence many of these nations adopted constitutions and bills of rights which followed the American (and French) examples. There is a strong resemblance, moreover, between the American Declaration of Independence of 1776 (obviously influenced by George Mason) and the Liberian Declaration of Independence of 1847. For a number of years Liberia was in effect an unofficial protectorate of the United States. But Mason's thinking had less of an impact at this time on other parts of the world: the Middle East, South Asia, and the Far East.

Turning to the Twentieth Century, many Americans looked upon World War I not just as a struggle between the Allies and the Central Powers, but also as a war to make the world safe for democracy. President Woodrow Wilson became the global leader of this idealistic crusade. Post-war developments, however, revealed this hope to be an unrealistic one. A quarter of a century later, two years after the outbreak of World War II in Europe, President Franklin Roosevelt and British Prime Minister Winston Churchill met off the coast of Newfoundland in August 1941, where they drew up the eight-part Atlantic Charter. Among its provisions were the right of people to choose their own form of government, and a peace of security after the war, with freedom from fear and want. Four months later the United States joined this conflict on the British side.

Shortly after the end of the fighting in Europe during April 1945, delegates from all over the world met at San Francisco to draw up a charter for the newly established United Nations. Franklin Roosevelt had just died, and Harry Truman was now President. On this occasion the United States agreed to join an international organization, unlike the situation after World War I, when the Senate had refused to approve American membership in the League of Nations.

One of the most important acts by the United Nations during its early years was to proclaim a Universal Declaration of Human Rights on December 10, 1948. There is no question but that certain passages from this document are quite similar in emphasis to the noble ideas expressed by George Mason in his Virginia Declaration of Rights. The first six articles from the United Nations document underscore this point:[15]

"Article 1. All human beings are born free and equal in dignity and rights. They are endowed with reason and conscience and should act towards another in a spirit of brotherhood.
Article 2. Everyone is entitled to all the rights and freedoms set forth in this declaration, without discrimination of any kind, such as race, color, sex, language, religion, political or other opinion, national or social origin, property, birth or other status.
Article 3. Everyone has the right to life, liberty and the security of person.
Article 4. No one shall be held in slavery or servitude; slavery and the slave trade shall be prohibited in all their forms.
Article 5. No one shall be subjected to torture or to cruel, inhuman or degrading treatment or punishment.
Article 6. Everyone has the right to recognition everywhere as a person before the law."

With respect to the other two dozen articles in the Universal Declaration of Human Rights, they guarantee to the individual such basic rights as protection against arbitrary arrest, a fair trial, the ownership of property, freedom from the arbitrary deprivation of the latter, meaningful participation by the individual in a government elected by the citizens, and freedom of thought, conscience, religion, press, and peaceful assembly and association.

In a contemporary statement Eleanor Roosevelt, who was

at that time the United States Representative to the General Assembly of the United Nations, compared the Universal Declaration of Human Rights to the French Declaration of the Rights of Man and the Citizen, and the first ten amendments to the American Constitution. Nowhere in her observations, though, is there any reference to George Mason, or even to Thomas Jefferson. Mrs. Roosevelt nevertheless did point out that American support for this declaration in general did not signify total acceptance of the provisions of all thirty articles. In her complaint about "the flagrant violation of human rights," moreover, she directed her attack at the Nazi and Fascist countries rather than at the equally guilty Communist ones, who certainly were not and are not in agreement with George Mason's Virginia Declaration of Rights. Marxists, it will be recalled, prefer for the government, not private individuals, to own property.

Since World War II such non-Western nations as Japan and India have moved towards a more democratic society recognizing human rights, but there remain scattered throughout the world a number of countries whose governments are authoritarian or even totalitarian in nature. One finds examples in Latin America as well as in Africa, in the Orient as well as in Eastern Europe. Not all of them are Communist-dominated, either, since quite a few are, or have been, under the rule of right-wing strong men who stay in power with the assistance of the military.

One may only wonder in closing how George Mason might react today from the standpoint of those liberties which he so vigorously championed two centuries ago. Would he support President Jimmy Carter's human rights crusade? Would he join Amnesty International, with its ban on capital punishment? Would he favor economic sanctions against apartheid-plagued South Africa? Would he have much trust in the United Nations, with its talkative General Assembly and its veto-hampered Security Council?

There is no question, however, that George Mason would look with favor upon the bills of rights and certain other provisions guaranteeing specific liberties which have been incorporated into many of the constitutions which nations around the world have adopted since the end of World War II. Some representative examples include those of France (1958), Venezuela (1961), the Egyptian complementary law number 37 (1972), Greece (1975), Spain (1978), and Nigeria (1979).[16] In practice such guarantees have perhaps been implemented rather imperfectly at times, but there is no question that the overall trend in recent years has been in the direction of safeguarding human rights. Hopefully one day their protection will at long last become universal.

Footnotes

1. Carl Becker, *The Declaration of Independence* (New York: Vintage Books, 1958). See p. 231.
2. R. R. Palmer, *The Age of the Democratic Revolution: A Political History of Europe and America, 1790-1800* (Princeton University Press, 1959). See p. 487. The author wishes to thank Professor Steven Reinhardt of the University of Texas at Arlington, History Department, for calling his attention to this volume.
3. Richard Morris, *The Emerging Nations and the American Revolution* (New York: Harper and Row, 1970). See p. 56.
4. George Mason III, "George Mason: Patriot," in *Northern Neck of Virginia Historical Magazine* (XXVI: December 1976). See pp. 2833.
5. George Walton Moore, "George Mason: The Statesman," in *Tyler's Quarterly Magazine* (XIV: April 1933). See pp. 223-4.
6. Armistead Churchill, *George Mason and the Bill of Rights*, four volumes, unpublished manuscript in the possession of the Virginia Historical Society, Richmond, Virginia. See II, 403-4. The author found the society's collection to be the outstanding source of Mason material – some of it quite rare – and he here acknowledges its vital importance to the composition of this essay.
7. John Hall Stewart, *A Documentary Survey of the French Revolution* (New York: The Macmillan Company, 1951). See pp. 113-4.
8. Palmer, pp. 520-1.
9. Robert A. Rutland, Editors, *The Papers of George Mason*, three volumes, (Chapel Hill: University of North Carolina Press, 1970). see III, 1171-72.
10. *Ibid.*, III, 1199.
11. *Ibid.*, III, 1216.
12. *Ibid.*, III, 1226.
13. Florette Henri, *George Mason of Virginia* (New York: Cromwell-Collier Press, 1971). See pp. 157-8.
14. Allen Johnson, et al, editor, *Dictionary of American Biography*, eleven volumes, (New York: Charles Scribners Sons, 1946-58). See VI, 363.
15. "Text of the Universal Declaration of Human Rights," in Department of State *Bulletin*, December 19, 1948. See p. 752.
16. There is a discussion of recent constitution-making abroad in Robert A. Goldwin and Art Kaufman, Editors, *Constitution Makers on Constitution Making: The Experience of Eight Nations* (Washington: American Enterprise Institute, 1988). For France, see pp. 29-31 and 51-2; for Greece, pp. 76-9 and 110; for Spain, pp. 260-1; for Egypt,

pp. 318-21; for Venezuela, pp. 374-7; and for Nigeria, pp. 427-9. This, of course, by no means exhausts the list of post-World war II foreign constitutions which openly endorse human rights in one form or another.

GEORGE MASON: WHY THE FORGOTTEN FOUNDING FATHER?

by Dr. Donald J. Senese

We should hope that the celebration of the bicentennial of the U.S. Constitution, and especially that of the Bill of Rights, should give us the opportunity for an awakened and renewed interest in George Mason, who remains in our history books the forgotten Founding Father. Mason certainly deserves the title commemorating one of the greatest contributions to our system of constitutional liberty — the "Father of the Bill of Rights."

The purpose of this study is to focus on some basic questions: why isn't George Mason better known? Why isn't he mentioned in the same breath as the other Founding Fathers as George Washington, James Madison, Thomas Jefferson — all Virginians — and Benjamin Franklin, Robert Morris, and Roger Sherman? Why can you watch an informative film on the making of the U.S. Constitution at the Visitor's Center in Philadelphia and hear not a mention of George Mason's name?

I maintain that this situation has occurred because of three reasons relating to the life of George Mason: one relating to his age; one to his political position; and one to his personal preferences.

The "Age Factor" is an important consideration. Mason was born in 1725 and by the time of the Constitutional Convention was already an elder statesman. Although he was not as old as Benjamin Franklin who was 81, he was not as young as James Madison at 36. Mason was 62 — he was 8 years older than George Washington and 18 years older than Thomas Jefferson. He was 26 years older than James Madison who achieved lasting fame as "the Father of the United States Constitution" because of the extensive notes he took during the debate and discussion of the formation of our Constitution, a chief source even today of those historic discussions.

Many of the Virginians associated with the Constitution were only on the eve of their greatest accomplishments in public service — George Washington and James Madison would go on to the presidency, John Marshall onto the U.S. Supreme Court as Chief Justice, Alexander Hamilton to the President's Cabinet as Secretary of the Treasury. These later accomplishments along with their service in the Constitutional Convention enhanced and established a lasting legacy and reputation for them. Mason was in the twilight of his years and his time for public service was coming to an end.

The "Political Factor" also played a significant role. George Mason's reputation would be influenced by the political stance he took on the adoption of the Constitution. He sought a defense of principles rather than the achievement of popularity. He had experience and wisdom and demonstrated his capacity for debate and invective during the deliberations of the Constitutional Convention.

And those who speak out in any society — championing ideas and challenging others — may fail to win popular acclaim while achieving distinction. He spoke often and eloquently at the Convention. He was not always on the popular, nor prevailing, side.

He was a delegate who had firm and determined opinions and he made these known to the delegates. His personality and statements sought at times to arouse and anger, rather than soothe and console.

Virginians played a prominent role in our independence and freedom and establishment as a nation. Thomas Jefferson is known as "the Father of the Declaration of Independence." George Washington has been correctly labeled as "the Father of Our Country" because of his service as the commander of our military forces in the Revolutionary War, the president of the Constitutional Convention, and our first President. And in this line of accolades, George Mason deserves the title "the Father of Our Bill of Rights."

Mason actively participated in the discussions of the Convention. Although he was an owner of slaves, he denounced the continuation of the slave trade and was disappointed that the new Constitution did not end this practice. He was fearful of a strong executive who could turn into a tyrant. Most of all, he was disappointed that the Constitution did not include a Declaration or Bill of Rights, a listing of rights guaranteed to the people and protected from the powers of government.

We read in political history of a conflict between champions of states rights versus individual rights. Mason was a champion of both — a central government of limited powers but one which provided protection of the rights of individual citizens.

When the Convention, which met from May through September of 1787, came to a conclusion and the time arrived for delegates to affix their signatures, Mason was one of only three who refused to sign it. He listed as foremost in his "Objections" to the Constitution the absence of a Bill of Rights. Mason's objections would be a strong influence for the arguments of the antifederalists in Virginia and other states in opposing the ratification of the Constitution.

The Constitutional Convention had provided that the Constitution could be ratified by the votes of 9 of the 13 states. New Hampshire became the ninth state to do so. However, two very important states had not done so — Virginia and New York — and the nation would undergo difficulty functioning without the assent of these two key states.

The fight in the Virginia Convention was especially intense, prolonged, and bitter. Some of the greatest statesmen of that age were arrayed on different sides of the debate on that document. James Madison and John Marshall strongly supported it. George Mason and Patrick Henry just as vehemently opposed it. Finally, the Virginia Convention ratified it by a margin of only ten votes, 89-79, on the promise that a Bill of Rights would be added to the Constitution when the First Congress met.

History is not kind to those who are on the losing side of great political arguments. The winners of political debates, like the victors in war, usually write the history of the event — kind to their allies and scornful of their opponents.

Mason refused to sign the Constitution and yet all except three signed it. In his home state, he opposed it and suffered a second defeat when the Virginia Convention ratified it — a prophet without honor in his own country. And these battles — so intense and so bitter that they tried the soul and intellect of the participants — had alienated him from longtime friends and associates.

Overall, Mason lost the battles but won the political war. When the First Congress met, a series of amendments to the Constitution was introduced, passed by Congress and sent to the states for ratification. The states ratified ten, which became the first ten amendments to the Constitution.

And this is how those essential freedoms we cherish today — the right of freedom of speech, freedom of assembly, freedom of the press, and freedom of religion, the right against self-incrimination, the right of trial by jury and protection against cruel and unusual punishment, the right to bear arms and the right against unlawful searches and seizures, and the right to have those powers not delegated to the federal government nor prohibited to the states remain with the people and the states — were added to the Constitution.

The Federalists had won and Mason, aligned with the antifederalists, had lost in the battle over the Constitution. Mason suffered the sting of defeat and retired to Gunston Hall.

The "Personal Factor" also played a role. George Mason's personal life was one free of excessive ambition and motivated by service to others. He was in many ways the reluctant statesman, who like Cincinnatus of Roman times, answered the call of his country for service, and then preferred to go back to the needs of his family and estate. He was left a widower with nine children, and he had extensive landholdings which he personally supervised and managed. He was occupied as both father and landowner.

He refused the call for service. He served but looked forward to returning to home and estate. When Senator William Grayson died on March 12, 1790, Governor Beverley Randolph appointed George Mason to the Senate but he refused because of health. This appointment eventually went to another aspiring Virginian, James Monroe.

We are talking about a period in our history of two hundred years ago — before radio, tape recorders, videotapes, and television.

Prominent individuals left their marks for posterity — and historical researchers — by their letters, public papers, speeches, diaries, and other similar materials.

Here we discover another contributing factor of why Mason is not better known. We lack the historical and written evidence we have of the other Founding Fathers.

For example, we have no recording or transcript of the debates in the Constitutional Convention, only the notes summarizing the speeches of Mason and others.

Mason, unlike Benjamin Franklin and Thomas Jefferson, did not write an autobiography.

Mason failed to keep a journal, similar to the one kept by George Washington and John Adams.

Mason did not publish articles and essays outlining his thoughts and views on government as did James Madison and Alexander Hamilton.

He gave speeches when he was a member of the Colonial Assembly of Virginia but no permanent records were kept of these speeches.

As for the post-Constitutional Convention activities, Mason, unlike Washington, Jefferson, Madison and Monroe, did not serve as president, and unlike Jefferson, Madison, and Hamilton, he did not serve in a president's cabinet.

The first biography of Mason came out about one hundred years after his death. Some of his most important papers were lost by fire. For George Washington, we may eventually have almost 100 volumes of his papers; for George Mason, we have only 3 volumes.

However, George Mason left a legacy in his leadership role and in the documents he contributed his ideas and his pen. He was a person of ideas. And ideas have consequences. Before the American Revolution even reached the bloody field of battle, the American Revolution had first taken place in the minds of men — in the realm of ideas and political concepts. And to this realm, Mason made a major contribution. The contribution stretched from the Fairfax Resolves to the Virginia Declaration of Rights to the eventual Bill of Rights added to the U.S. Constitution.

The Bill of Rights became part of our Constitution in December of 1791. Less than a year later, George Mason died at Gunston Hall Plantation on October 7, 1792. He had been victorious in a cause that did eventually triumph — he had witnessed before his death the addition of the Bill of Rights to the U.S. Constitution.

We know in retrospect the great influence this Bill of Rights had on the evolution of our constitutional history and the influence it has — and still does exercise — over other nations over the two centuries of its existence.

The celebration of the bicentennial of the U.S. Constitution continues until 1991 with the commemoration of the ratification of the Bill of Rights.

And although Mason was on the losing side of the battle over the ratification of the Constitution, the objections he brought up did become part of other discussions and debates over our Constitution and its interpretation throughout our history. We should not let his defeat on that issue obscure the great contributions he made by first putting in words the great body of rights we possess — words found in the Virginia Declaration of Rights, echoed in the Declaration of Independence, and enshrined in the U.S. Bill of Rights.

George Mason remains an American hero, a Founding Father who contributed much to the Constitution we celebrate. Mason provided that ideas have consequences as he left us one of our most enduring constitutional legacies — the Bill of Rights.

GEORGE MASON AND THE LEGACY OF CONSTITUTIONAL LIBERTY

An Examination of the Influence of George Mason on the American Bill of Rights

Section 4: Appendices — Documents Protecting Individual Rights

"Final Draft of the Virginia Declaration of Rights"

"Objections to this Constitution of Government" by George Mason

United States: "Bill of Rights, U.S. Constitution"

France: "Declaration of the Rights of Man and the Citizen"

United Nations: "Universal Declaration of Human Rights"

FINAL DRAFT OF THE VIRGINIA DECLARATION OF RIGHTS

[12 June 1776]

A DECLARATION OF RIGHTS made by the Representatives of the good people of VIRGINIA, assembled in full and free Convention; which rights do pertain to (them and their) posterity, as the basis and foundation of Government.

1. That all men are (by nature) equally free and independent, and have certain inherent rights, of which, (when they enter into a state of society,) they cannot, by any compact, deprive or divest their posterity; (namely,) the enjoyment of life and liberty, with the means of acquiring and possessing property, and pursuing and obtaining happiness and safety.

2. That all power is vested in, and consequently derived from, the People; that magistrates are their trustees and servants, and at all times amenable to them.

3. That Government is, or ought to be, instituted for the common benefit, protection, and security of the people, nation, or community; — of all the various modes and forms of Government that is best which is capable of producing the greatest degree of happiness and safety, and is most effectually secured against the danger of mal-administration; — and that, whenever any Government shall be found inadequate or contrary to these purposes, a majority of the community hath an indubitable, unalienable, and indefeasible right, to reform, alter, or abolish it, in such manner as shall be judged most conducive to the publick weal.

4. That no man, or set of men, are entitled to exclusive or separate emoluments and privileges from the community, but in consideration of publick services; which, not being descendible, (neither ought the offices) of Magistrate, Legislator, or Judge, (to be hereditary).

5. That the Legislative and Executive powers of the

State should be separate and distinct from the Judicative; and, that the members of the two first may be restrained from oppression, by feeling and participating the burdens of the people, they should, at fixed periods, be reduced to a private station, return into that body from which they were originally taken, and the vacancies be supplied by frequent, certain, and regular elections, (in which all, or any part of the former members, to be again eligible, or ineligible, as the law shall direct).

6. That elections of members to serve as Representatives of the people, in Assembly, ought to be free; and that all men, having sufficient evidence of permanent common interest with, and attachment to, the community, have the right of suffrage, (and cannot be taxed or deprived of their property for) publick uses without their own consent or that of their Representative (so elected,) nor bound by any law to which they have not, in like manner, assented, for the publick good.

7. That all power of suspending laws, or the execution of laws, by any authority, without consent of the Representatives of the people, is injurious to their rights, and ought not to be exercised.

8. That in all capital or criminal prosecutions a man hath a right to demand the cause and nature of his accusation, to be confronted with the accusers and witnesses, to call for evidence in his favour, and to a speedy trial by an impartial jury of his vicinage, without whose unanimous consent he cannot be found guilty, nor can he be compelled to give evidence against himself; that no man be deprived of his liberty except by the law of the land, or the judgment of his peers.

9. That excessive bail ought not to be required, nor excessive fines imposed, nor cruel and unusual punishments inflicted.

10. That (general) warrants, whereby any officer or messenger may be commanded to search suspected places (without evidence of a fact committed,) or to seize any person or persons (not named, or whose offence is) not particularly

described (and supported by evidence,) are grievous and oppressive, and ought not to be granted.

11. That in controversies respecting property, and in suits between man and man, the ancient trial by Jury is preferable to any other, and ought to be held sacred.

12. That the freedom of the Press is one of the greatest bulwarks of liberty, and can never be restrained but by despotick Governments.

13. That a well-regulated Militia, composed of the body of the people, trained to arms, is the proper, natural, and safe defence of a free State; that Standing Armies, in time of peace, should be avoided as dangerous to liberty; and that, in all cases, the military should be under strict subordination to, and governed by, the civil power.

14. That the people have a right to uniform Government; and, therefore, that no Government separate from, or independent of, the Government of *Virginia*, ought to be erected or established within the limits thereof.

15. That no free Government, or the blessing of liberty, can be preserved to any people but by firm adherence to justice, moderation, temperance, frugality, and virtue, and by frequent recurrence to fundamental principles.

16. That Religion, or the duty which we owe to our *Creator*, and the manner of discharging it, can be directed only by reason and conviction, not by force or violence; and, therefore, all men (are equally entitled to the free) exercise of religion, according to the dictates of conscience; and that it is the mutual duty of all to practise Christian forbearance, love, and charity, towards each other.

OBJECTIONS TO THIS CONSTITUTION OF GOVERNMENT

by George Mason

There is no Declaration of Rights, and the laws of the general government being paramount to the laws and constitution of the several States, the Declarations of Rights in the separate States are no security. Nor are the people secured even in the enjoyment of the benefit of the common law.

In the House of Representatives there is not the substance but the shadow only of representation; which can never produce proper information in the legislature, or inspire confidence in the people; the laws will therefore be generally made of men little concerned in, and unacquainted with their effects and consequences.

The Senate have the power of altering all money bills, and of originating appropriations of money, and the salaries of the officers of their own appointment, in conjunction with the president of the United States, although they are not the representatives of the people or amendable to them.

These with their other great powers, viz.: their power in the appointment of ambassadors and all public officers, in making treaties, and in trying all impeachments, their influence upon and connection with the supreme Executive from these causes, their duration of office and their being a constantly existing body, almost continually sitting, joined with their being one complete branch of the legislature, will destroy any balance in the government, and enable them to accomplish what usurpations they please upon the rights and liberties of the people.

The Judiciary of the United States is so constructed and extended, as to absorb and destroy the judiciaries of the several States; thereby rendering law as tedious, intricate and expensive, and justice as unattainable, by a great part of the community, as in England, and enabling the rich to oppress and ruin the poor.

The President of the United States has no Constitutional Council, a thing unknown in any safe and regular government. He will therefore be unsupported by proper information and advice, and will generally be directed by minions and favorites; or he will become a tool to the Senate — or a Council of State will grow out of the principal officers of the great departments; the worst and most dangerous of all ingredients for such a council in a free country; From this fatal defect has arisen the improper power of the Senate in the appointment of public officers, and the alarming dependence and connection between that branch of the legislature and the supreme Executive.

Hence also sprung that unnecessary officer the Vice-President, who for want of other employment is made president of the Senate, thereby dangerously blending the executive and legislative powers, besides always giving to some one of the States an unnecessary and unjust pre-eminence over the others.

The President of the United States has the unrestrained power of granting pardons for treason, which may be sometimes exercised to screen from punishment those whom he had secretly instigated to commit the crime, and thereby prevent a discovery of his own guilt.

By declaring all treaties supreme laws of the land, the Executive and the Senate have, in many cases, an exclusive power of legislation; which might have been avoided by proper distinctions with respect to treaties, and requiring the assent of the House of Representatives, where it could be done with safety.

By requiring only a majority to make all commercial and navigation laws, the five Southern States, whose produce and circumstances are totally different from that of the eight Northern and Eastern States, may be ruined, for such rigid and premature regulations may be made as will enable the merchants of the Northern and Eastern States not only to demand an exorbitant freight, but to monopolize the purchase of the commodities at their own price, for many years, to the great injury of the landed interest, and impoverishment of the people; and the danger is the greater as the gain on one side will be in proportion to the loss on the other. Whereas requiring two-thirds of the members present in both Houses would have produced mutual moderation, promoted the general interest, and removed an insuperable objection to the adoption of this government.

Under their own construction of the general clause, at the end of the enumerated powers, the Congress may grant monopolies in trade and commerce, constitute new crimes, inflict unusual and severe punishments, and extend their powers as far as they shall think proper; so that the State legislatures have no security for the powers now presumed to remain to them, or the people for their rights.

There is no declaration of any kind, for preserving the liberty of the press, or the trial by jury in civil causes; nor against the danger of standing armies in time of peace.

The State legislatures are restrained from laying export duties on their own produce.

Both the general legislature and the State legislature are expressly prohibited making *ex post facto* laws; though there never was nor can be a legislature but must and will make such laws, when necessity and the public safety require them; which will hereafter be a breach of all the constitutions in the Union, and afford precedents for other innovations.

This government will set out a moderate aristocracy: it is at present impossible to foresee whether it will, in its operation, produce a monarchy, or a corrupt, tyrannical aristocracy; it will most probably vibrate some years between the two, and then terminate in the one or the other.

The general legislature is restrained from prohibiting the further importation of slaves for twenty odd years; though such importations render the United States weaker, more vulnerable, and less capable of defence.

BILL OF RIGHTS, U.S. CONSTITUTION

Article I
Congress shall make no law respecting an establishment of religion, or prohibiting the free exercise thereof; or abridging the freedom of speech, or of the press; or the right of the people peaceably to assemble, and to petition the Government for a redress of grievances.

Article II
A well regulated Militia, being necessary to the security of a free State, the right of the people to keep and bear Arms, shall not be infringed.

Article III
No Soldier shall, in time of peace be quartered in any house, without the consent of the Owner, nor in time of war, but in a manner to be prescribed by law.

Article IV
The rights of the people to be secure in their persons, houses, papers, and effects, against unreasonable searches and seizures, shall not be violated, and no Warrants shall issue, but upon probable cause, supported by Oath or affirmation, and particularly describing the place to be searched, and the persons or things to be seized.

Article V
No person shall be held to answer for a capital, or otherwise infamous crime, unless on a presentment or indictment of a Grand Jury, except in cases arising in the land or naval forces, or in the Militia, when in actual service in time of War or public danger; nor shall any person be subject for the same offense to be twice put in jeopardy of life or limb; nor shall be compelled in any Criminal Case to be a witness against himself, nor be deprived of life, liberty, or property,

without due process of law; nor shall private property be taken for public use, without just compensation.

Article VI
In all criminal prosecutions, the accused shall enjoy the right to a speedy and public trial, by an impartial jury of the State and district wherein the crime shall have been committed, which district shall have been previously ascertained by law, and to be informed of the nature and cause of the accusation; to be confronted with the witnesses against him; to have compulsory process for obtaining witnesses in his favor, and to have the Assistance of Counsel for his defense.

Article VII
In Suits at common law, where the value in controversy shall exceed twenty dollars, the right of trial by jury shall be preserved, and no fact tried by a jury, shall be otherwise re-examined in any Court of the United States than according to the rules of the common law.

Article VIII
Excessive bail shall not be required, nor excessive fines imposed, nor cruel and unusual punishments inflicted.

Article IX
The enumeration in the Constitution, of certain rights, shall not be construed to deny or disparage others retained by the people.

Article X
The powers not delegated to the United States by the Constitution, nor prohibited by it to the States, are reserved to the States respectively, or to the people.

DECLARATION OF THE RIGHTS OF MAN AND THE CITIZEN

Article 1
Men are born and remain free and equal in respect of rights. Social distinctions shall be based solely upon public utility.

Article 2
The purpose of all civil associations is the preservation of the natural and imprescriptible rights of man. These rights are liberty, property and resistance to oppression.

Article 3
The nation is essentially the source of all sovereignty, nor shall any body of men or any individual exercise authority which is not expressly derived from it.

Article 4
Liberty consists in the power of doing whatever does not injure another. Accordingly the exercise of the natural rights of every man has not other limits than those which are necessary to secure to every other man the free exercise of the same rights; and these limits are determinable only by the law.

Article 5
The law ought to prohibit only actions hurtful to society. What is not prohibited by the law should not be hindered; nor should any one be compelled to do that which the law does not require.

Article 6
The law is an expression of the common will. All citizens have a right to concur, either personally or by their representation in its formation. It should be the same for all, whether it protects or punishes; and all being equal in its

sight, are equally eligible to all honours, places and employments, according to their different abilities, without any other distinction than that of their virtues and talents.

Article 7
No one shall be accused, arrested or imprisoned, save in the cases determined by law, and according to the forms which it has prescribed. All who solicit, promote, execute, or cause to be executed, arbitrary orders, ought to be punished, and every citizen summoned or apprehended by virtue of the law, ought immediately to obey, and becomes culpable if he resists.

Article 8
The law should impose only such penalties as are absolutely and evidently necessary; and no one ought to be punished but by virtue of a law promulgated before the offence, and legally applied.

Article 9
Every man being counted innocent until he has been convicted, whenever his arrest becomes indispensable, all vigour more than is necessary to his person ought to be provided against by law.

Article 10
No man is to be interfered with because of his opinions, not even because of religious opinions, provided his avowal of them does not disturb public order as established by law.

Article 11
The unrestrained communication of thoughts or opinions being one of the most precious rights of man, every citizen may speak, write and publish freely, provided he be responsible for the abuse or this liberty, in the cases determined by law.

Article 12
A public force being necessary to give security to the rights

of men and of citizens, that force is instituted for the benefit of the community, and not for the particular benefit of the person to whom it is entrusted.

Article 13
A common contribution being necessary for the support of the public force, and for defraying the other expenses of government, it should be divided equally among the members of the community, according to their abilities.

Article 14
Every citizen has a right, either of himself or his representative, to a free voice in determining the necessity of public contributions, the appropriation of them, and their amount, mode of assessment, and duration.

Article 15
The community has the right to demand of all its agents an account of their conducts.

Article 16
Every community in which a security of rights and separation of powers is not provided for needs a constitution.

Article 17
The right to property being inviolable and secured, no one shall be deprived of it, except in cases of evident public necessity; legally ascertained, and on condition of a previous just indemnity.

UNITED NATIONS: UNIVERSAL DECLARATION OF HUMAN RIGHTS

Preamble

Whereas recognition of the inherent dignity and of the equal and inalienable rights of all members of the human family is the foundation of freedom, justice and peace in the world,

Whereas disregard and contempt for human rights have resulted in barbarous acts which have outraged the conscience of mankind, and the advent of a world in which human beings shall enjoy freedom of speech and belief and freedom from fear and want has been proclaimed as the highest aspiration of the common people,

Whereas it is essential, if man is not to be compelled to have recourse, as a last resort, to rebellion against tyranny and oppression, that human rights should be protected by the rule of law,

Whereas it is essential to promote the development of friendly relations between nations,

Whereas the peoples of the United Nations have in the Charter reaffirmed their faith in fundamental human rights, in the dignity and worth of the human person and in the equal rights of men and women and have determined to promote social progress and better standards of life in larger freedom,

Whereas Member States have pledged themselves to achieve, in cooperation with the United Nations, the promotion of universal respect for and observance of human rights and fundamental freedoms.

Whereas a common understanding of these rights and freedoms is of the greatest importance for the full realization of this pledge.

Now, Therefore,

THE GENERAL ASSEMBLY

proclaims

This universal declaration of human rights as a common standard of achievement for all peoples and all nations, to the end that every individual and every organ of society, keeping this Declaration constantly in mind, shall strive by teaching and education to promote respect for these rights and freedoms and by progressive measures, national and international, to secure their universal and effective recognition and observance, both among the peoples of Member States themselves and among the peoples of territories under their jurisdiction.

Article 1
All human beings are born free and equal in dignity and rights. They are endowed with reason and conscience and should act towards one another in a spirit of brotherhood.

Article 2
Everyone is entitled to all rights and freedoms set forth in this Declaration, without distinction of any kind, such as race, colour, sex, language, religion, political or other opinion, national or social origin, property, birth or other status.
  Furthermore, no distinction shall be made on the basis of the political, jurisdictional or international status of the country or territory to which a person belongs, whether it be independent, trust, non-self-governing or under any other limitation of sovereignty.

Article 3
Everyone has the right to life, liberty and security of person.

Article 4
No one shall be held in slavery or servitude; slavery and the

slave trade shall be prohibited in all their forms.

Article 5
No one shall be subjected to torture or to cruel, inhuman or degrading treatment or punishment.

Article 6
Everyone has the right to recognition everywhere as a person before the law.

Article 7
All are equal before the law and are entitled without any discrimination to equal protection of the law. All are entitled to equal protection against any discrimination in violation of this Declaration and against any incitement to such discrimination.

Article 8
Everyone has the right to an effective remedy by the competent national tribunals for acts violating the fundamental rights granted him by the constitution or by law.

Article 9
No one shall be subjected to arbitrary arrest, detention or exile.

Article 10
Everyone is entitled in full equality to a fair and public hearing by an independent and impartial tribunal, in the determination of his rights and obligations and of any criminal charge against him.

Article 11
1. Everyone charged with a penal offence has the right to be presumed innocent until proved guilty according to law in a public trial at which he has had all the guarantees necessary for his defense.

2. No one shall be held guilty of any penal offense on account of any act or omission which did not constitute a penal offence, under national or international law, at the time when it was committed. Nor shall a heavier penalty, be imposed than the one that was applicable at the time the penal offence was committed.

Article 12
No one shall be subjected to arbitrary interference with his privacy, family, home or correspondence, nor to attacks upon his honour and reputation. Everyone has the right to the protection of the law against such interference or attacks.

Article 13
1. Everyone has the right to freedom of movement and residence within the borders of each state.
2. Everyone has the right to leave any country, including his own, and to return to his country.

Article 14
1. Everyone has the right to seek and to enjoy in other countries asylum from persecution.
2. This right may not be invoked in the case of prosecutions genuinely arising from non-political crimes or from acts contrary to the purposes and principles of the United Nations.

Article 15
1. Everyone has the right to a nationality.
2. No one shall be arbitrarily deprived of his nationality nor denied the right to change his nationality.

Article 16
1. Men and women of full age, without any limitation due to race, nationality or religion, have the right to marry and to found a family. They are entitled to equal rights as to marriage, during marriage and at its dissolution.
2. Marriage shall be entered into only with the free and full

consent of the intending spouses.

3. The family is the natural and fundamental group unit of society and is entitled to protection by society and the State.

Article 17
1. Everyone has the right to own property alone as well as in association with others.
2. No one shall be arbitrarily deprived of his property.

Article 18
Everyone has the right to freedom of thought, conscience and religion; this right includes freedom to change his religion or belief, and freedom, either alone or in community with others and in public or private, to manifest his religion or belief in teaching, practice, worship and observance.

Article 19
Everyone has the right to freedom of opinion and expression; this right includes freedom to hold opinions without interference and to see, receive and impart information and ideas through any media and regardless of frontiers.

Article 20
1. Everyone has the right to freedom of peaceful assembly and association.
2. No one may be compelled to belong to an association.

Article 21
1. Everyone has the right to take part in the government of his country, directly or through freely chosen representatives.
2. Everyone has the right of equal access to public service in his country.
3. The will of the people shall be the basis of the authority of government; this will shall be expressed in periodic and genuine elections which shall be of universal and equal suffrage and shall be held by secret vote or by equivalent free voting procedures.

Article 22
Everyone, as a member of society, has the right to social security and is entitled to realization, through national effort and international co-operation and in accordance with the organization and resources of each State, of the economic, social and cultural rights indispensable for his dignity and the free development of his personality.

Article 23
1. Everyone has the right to work, to free choice of employment, to just and favorable conditions of work and to protection against unemployment.
2. Everyone, without any discrimination, has the right to equal pay for equal work.
3. Everyone who works has the right to just and favorable remuneration ensuring for himself and his family an existence worthy of human dignity, and supplemented, if necessary, by other means of social protection.
4. Everyone has the right to form and to join trade unions for the protection of his interests.

Article 24
Everyone has the right to rest and leisure, including reasonable limitation of working hours and periodic holidays with pay.

Article 25
1. Everyone has the right to a standard or living adequate for the health and well-being or himself and of his family, including food, clothing, housing and medical care and necessary social services, and the right to security in the event of unemployment, sickness, disability, widowhood, old age or other lack of livelihood in circumstances beyond his control.
2. Motherhood and childhood are entitled to special care and assistance. All children, whether born in or out of wedlock, shall enjoy the same social protection.

Article 26
1. Everyone has the right to education. Education shall be free, at least in the elementary and fundamental stages. Elementary education shall be compulsory. Technical and professional education shall be made generally available and higher education shall be equally accessible to all on the basis of merit.
2. Education shall be directed to the full development of the human personality and to the strengthening of respect for human rights and fundamental freedoms. It shall promote understanding, tolerance and friendship among all nations, racial or religious groups, and shall further the activities of the United Nations for the maintenance of peace.
3. Parents have a prior right to choose the kind of education that shall be given to their children.

Article 27
1. Everyone has the right freely to participate in the cultural life of the community, to enjoy the arts and to share in scientific advancement and its benefits.
2. Everyone has the right to the protection of the moral and material interests resulting from any scientific, literary or artistic production of which he is the author.

Article 28
Everyone is entitled to a social and international order in which the rights and freedoms set forth in this Declaration can be fully realized.

Article 29
1. Everyone has duties to the community in which alone the free and full development of his personality, is possible.
2. In the exercise of his rights and freedoms, everyone shall be subject only to such limitations as are determined by law solely for the purpose of securing due recognition and respect for the rights and freedoms of others and of meeting the just requirements of morality, public order and the general welfare in a democratic society.

3. These rights and freedoms may in no case be exercised contrary to the purposes and principles of the United Nations.

Article 30
Nothing in this Declaration may be interpreted as implying for any State, group or person any right to engage in any activity or to perform any act aimed at the destruction of any of the rights and freedoms set forth herein.

"George Mason Statue on the grounds of Capital Square, Richmond, Virginia"
Photograph by Charles Baptie

"George Mason"

"Portraits of George and Ann Mason by Dominic W. Boudet, c. 1811, copied from the 1750 originals by John Hesselius." Courtesy of the Virginia Museum of Fine Arts, Richmond, Virginia.
Gift of David K. E. Bruce

"Ann Mason"

"Landfront of Gunston Hall, the home of George Mason"
Courtesy of the Board of Regents, Gunston Hall.

"Sketch of Gunston Hall, c. 1840, home of George Mason"
Courtesy of the Board of Regents, Gunston Hall

"Garden and Grounds of Gunston Hall"
"Center Hall of Gunston Hall"
Photograph courtesy of the Board of Regents, Gunston Hall.

"Etching of George Mason" by Albert Rosenthal, 1888
Courtesy of the Board of Regents, Gunston Hall

Dr. Edward W. Chester was born in Richmond, Virginia and presently serves as Professor of American Political History at the University of Texas at Arlington, Texas. He received his A.B. Degree from Morris Harvey College (summa cum laude), now the University of Charleston, and his M.A. degree and his Ph.D. degrees from the University of Pittsburgh, all in history. He has taught at Arlington since 1965, where he has offered courses in American political parties and American political thought. Dr. Chester has received grants from the Earhart Foundation, and has presented papers at numerous historical meetings. He is the author of *Issues and Responses in State Political Experience; Radio, Television, and American Politics*; and *A Guide to Political Platforms*, and various political articles. Dr. Chester is currently working on a history of mid-term elections in the U.S. since the Second World War.

Dr. Robert P. Davidow was born in Detroit, Michigan and presently is Professor of Law at the George Mason University School of Law (Arlington, Virginia). Dr. Davidow received his A.B. degree from Dartmouth College (magna cum laude), J.D. from the University of Michigan, his LL.M. from Harvard University, and his J.S.D. from Columbia University. He practiced law in a law firm in Cleveland, Ohio, with the Judge Advocate General's Corps of the U.S. Army and as Special Assistant to the Public Defender in Tallahassee, Florida. He has taught at the University of North Dakota School of Law, Florida State University College of Law, and Texas Tech University School of Law. Dr. Davidow has published numerous articles in law journals including the *North Carolina Law Review, Texas Law Review, Case Western Reserve Law Review*, and the *University of Cincinnati Law Review* and served as editor of the book *Natural Rights and Natural Law: The Legacy of George Mason*.

Mr. Joseph Horrell was born in Atlanta, Missouri, and presently lives in retirement in Lexington, Virginia. He received his B. A. degree from Murray State University (Kentucky) and his M.A. degree from Vanderbilt University and did additional graduate work at the University of North Carolina where he also served as an instructor in English. He served as an officer in the U.S. Navy 1941-1946. He then attended and graduated from Jesus College, Cambridge receiving a B.A. (First Class) in English Literature, M. Litt., and M.A.; he was a Fulbright scholar at the college. He has taught at St. John's College (Annapolis, Maryland), and at St. John's, Pembroke, Emmanuel and King's Colleges, all a part of Cambridge University. He entered private business spending twenty-five years with the Vitro Corporation. After retiring from the senior management at Vitro, he started research on colonial history with a specialization in the Virginia Constitution, 1619-1776. He is consulting editor to *The Papers of George Washington* (Colonial Series) on the settlement on the Custis estate.

Sandra Day O'Connor was born in El Paso, Texas and presently serves as an Associate Justice of the United States Supreme Court. She received her B.A. degree (magna cum laude) and her LL.B. degree both from Stanford University where she was a member of the Order of the Coif, and the Board of Editors, *Stanford Law Review*. She served as Deputy County Attorney in San Mateo County, California, engaged in the private practice of law in Maryvale, Arizona, and served as the Assistant Attorney General in Arizona. She was appointed State Senator and won re-election twice serving from 1969-1975. She was elected Senate Majority Leader in 1972. Justice O'Connor won election as judge of the Maricopa County Superior Court, Phoenix, Arizona, later was appointed to the Arizona Court of Appeals and was nominated to the U.S. Supreme Court by President Ronald Reagan in 1981. She was confirmed by the U.S. Senate and took her oath of office on September 25, 1981. She became the first woman to serve on the U.S. Supreme Court.

Dr. Josephine F. Pacheco was born in Richmond, Virginia, and is presently Professor of History and Director of the Center for the Study of Constitutional Rights at George Mason University (Fairfax, Virginia). She received a B.A. degree from Westhampton College of the University of Richmond (Virginia) and the M.A. and Ph.D. degrees from the University of Chicago. She has taught at Howard University and the Northern Virginia Center of the University of Virginia. Dr. Pacheco has taught at George Mason University for 21 years and has authored *The Problem of Racism in the United States*; co-authored *Three Who Dared*; and edited *The Legacy of George Mason*. She is a member of the Virginia Commission on the Bicentennial of the United States Constitution and the Fairfax County Commission on the Bicentennial of the United States Constitution.

Dr. Diane D. Pikcunas was born in Washington, D. C. and presently serves as the Principal of Komensky Elementary School in Berwyn, Illinois and Adjunct Professor of Education at the National College of Education in Lombard, Ill.. She received her B.S. degree from Ill. State University (Normal, Ill.), a Masters of Science in Education with a specialization in the area of Learning Disabilities and a Doctorate in Education with a specialization in Supervision and Curriculum, both from Northern Illinois Univ. (DeKalb, Ill.). Dr. Pikcunas has published articles in *The World and I, International Schools Journal, International Quarterly, The Principal, Universitas,* and *The Journal of Social, Political and Economic Studies*. She has had three of her writings published in the *U.S Congressional Record*. Dr. Pikcunas serves on the Advisory Board of the National Center for Presidential Research (Washington, D.C.) and is a member of the National Speaker's Bureau of the U.S. Commission on the Bicentennial of the U.S. Constitution. Active in various activities commemorating the bicentennial, her speech "The U.S. Constitution: 'The Morning After'" was published in *Vital Speeches of the Day* and won her in 1988 the George Washington Honor Medal for Excellence in the category of Public Communication from the Freedoms Foundation of Valley Forge, Valley Forge, PA. She serves as the Publicity Chairman for the Delta Epsilson Chapter of Kappa Delta Pi, and as a member of the Illinois Principals Association and the Gunston Hall Neighbors Association.

Dr. Robert A. Rutland was born in Okmulgee, Oklahoma and is presently Research Professor of history at the University of Tulsa. He received his B.A. degree from the University of Oklahoma, his M.A. from Cornell University and his Ph.D. degree from Vanderbilt University. He served on the faculty of the University of California at Los Angeles 1954-1969 and was the coordinator for the bicentennial program at the Library of Congress 1969-1971. He is the author of numerous books including *Birth of the Bill of Rights, George Mason: Reluctant Statesman, Ordeal of the Constitution,* and *George Mason and the War for Independence.* He edited *The Papers of George Mason* (3 volumes) and served as the editor-in-chief of *The Papers of James Madison* (until 1986) at the University of Virginia. His *George Mason: Reluctant Statesman* will be brought out in a new edition in 1989.

Dr. Donald J. Senese was born in Chicago, Illinois and presently serves as a public policy consultant in Washington, D. C. He received his Bachelor's Degree from Loyola University and his Masters and Doctorate from the University of South Carolina, all in history. He specialized in United States constitutional and political history before 1860 with a secondary field in Asian history (China, Japan, and Korea). He served as an Associate Professor of History at Radford University (Radford, Virginia), worked on Capitol Hill for eight years (for Members of the U.S. House of Representatives and the U.S. Senate) and was appointed by President Ronald Reagan to serve as the Assistant Secretary for Educational Research and Improvement, U.S. Education Department (1981-1985). He is the author of five books including *Democracy in Mainland China: The Myth and the Reality* and over fifty articles on public policy issues; he is the editor of *Ideas Confront Reality: An Analysis of Critical Issues in the Reagan Era* and has contributed chapters to other works. He authored "George Mason and the Bill of Rights," a reprint of his two articles from the *Fairfax Chronicles* and published in pamphlet by the Fairfax County Bicentennial Commission. Dr. Senese has twice received awards from the Freedoms Foundation of Valley Forge, Valley Forge, Pennsylvania, and was selected as One of the Outstanding Young Men of America by the Jaycees in both 1976 and 1978. He serves as the Director of the National Center for Presidential Research, vice chairman of the Fairfax County History Commission, and a member of the Fairfax County Commission on the Bicentennial of the United States Constitution.

Index

Adam, Robert 49
Adams, John 15, 79, 129, 131, 151
Adamson v. California 109
Africa 144
Alexander, Charles 49, 50, 57
Alexandria 34-38, 40, 42-44, 46, 48, 49, 56, 57, 58, 82
Allied Structural Steel Co. v. Spannaus 99
American Revolution 16, 20, 29, 56, 57, 58, 128, 130, 145, 152
Amnesty International 144
Annapolis 61, 62, 117
Annapolis Conference 61
Anti-Federalists 59, 93, 103, 104, 111, 118
Arell, David 49, 57
aristocracy 18, 19, 29, 69, 73, 78, 105, 118, 160
Articles of Confederation 24, 55, 61, 63, 67, 104
assembly, freedom of 150, 161
Austria-Hungary 141
Baltimore 62, 111
Barron v. Mayor of Baltimore 111
Bastille 135
Bill of Rights 15, 16, 24, 29-31, 41, 42, 45, 46, 49, 53, 55
                        72, 73, 75, 78-81, 85, 88, 89, 91, 93-95, 97
                        102-104, 109, 111, 118-121, 123-127
                        131, 133, 134, 140, 141, 145, 147-149, 152, 161
Bill of Rights (U.S.) 161-162
Black, Justice Hugo 109
Blair, John 62, 117
Brandywine, Battle of 130
Brazil 140
Brennan, Justice William 107, 120
Brent, Sarah 23
Broadwater, Charles 35, 40, 45, 48-50, 52, 56, 57
Brown v. Board of Education 109
Brown, William 49, 50
Buckland, William 21
Butler, Justice Pierce 99
Byrd family 19
Calhoun, John C. 72
capital punishment 95, 144
Carter, Jimmy 144
checks and balances 86, 89, 91, 94, 103
Chichester, Richard 48, 49
church and state 121, 122
Churchill, Armistead 134, 145
Churchill, Winston 142
Cicero 87
Cincinnatus 150

Cockburn, Martin 48, 49
Cockburn family 20
Coke, Sir Edward 66, 87, 124
Colonial Assembly of Virginia 151
Committee of Eleven 119
Committee of Public Safety 139
Committee on Propositions and Grievances 38, 51
Committee of Style 77
Common Law 54, 77, 107, 111, 158, 162
Congressional control over the militia 65
Constitution ... 15, 16, 20, 24, 27-29, 32, 34, 40, 41, 43, 45-47, 51-53
  57, 61-63, 67, 71-81, 83-85, 88, 89, 91-94, 96, 97, 99-107
  110-113, 117, 118, 120, 122, 126, 136, 137
  141, 144, 145, 147-150, 152, 158, 161, 162, 165, 168
Constitutional Convention of 1787 .... 84, 139
Constitutional Council 77, 159
Continental Congress 23, 24, 40, 104
Council, The 19, 35-37, 39-41, 44-46, 49, 53, 56, 63, 107
Council of Revision 69, 89, 91, 102, 105
Crown Law 133
cruel and unusual punishment 99, 107, 150
Cuba 140
Dade, Baldwin 52
Dante 133
death penalty 94, 99
death 21, 22, 35, 42, 53, 82, 106, 107, 131
Declaration of Rights of Man and the Citizen .. 128, 137, 139, 161-165
Declaration of Rights, Virginia 23-27, 29, 30, 40, 54, 62, 67, 72
  75, 77-79, 81, 83, 84, 87-89, 99, 106, 108, 110, 111
  117, 119, 121, 124, 126, 128-130, 132-135
  137-139, 141-144, 155-157
Deneale, George 52
Denmark 140, 141
Dinwiddie, Governor 36, 37
Doeg Neck 20
Dryden, John 133
due process of law 109, 124, 125, 162
Dulaney, Benjamin 49
Duncan v. Louisiana 109
Eastern Europe 144
Egyptian complementary law 145
Eighth Amendment 125, 126, 162
Eleventh Amendment 120
Ellsworth, Oliver 78, 102, 112
England . 17, 19, 21, 54, 68, 89, 102, 124, 128, 131, 133, 139, 141, 159
English Bill of Rights 126
Everson v. Board of Education 122
executive power .. 26, 36, 45, 47, 54, 56, 63, 65, 66, 69, 71, 77, 87, 90
  91, 136, 149, 155, 158, 159

"Extracts of Virginia Charters" 23
Fairfax County Court 33, 53, 55, 98
Fairfax County Resolves 23, 40, 81, 102, 117, 152
Fairfax County 15, 20, 22, 23, 30, 31, 117
             33, 34, 37, 40, 42, 45, 47, 50-53, 55, 56, 57, 98, 102
Fairfax County Committee of Safety 23
Fairfax Independent Company 58, 87
father of the Bill of Rights 147
fear, freedom from 142, 166
Federalists 58, 75, 79, 80, 93, 103, 104, 110, 111, 118, 119, 150
Fifth Amendment 106, 109, 161-162
Final Draft of the Virginia Constitution of 1776 57
First Amendment 30, 121-124, 161
First Congress 79, 80, 94, 125, 149, 150
Fitzgerald, John 49
Founding Fathers 21, 27, 28, 32, 55, 59, 122, 147, 151
Fourteenth Amendment 95, 109, 123-125
Fowkes, Guy 21
France 17, 38, 128-133, 136, 138, 139, 141, 145
Franco-American Alliance of 1778 131
Franklin, Benjamin 15, 76, 103, 118, 128, 129, 132, 147, 151
Frankfurter, Justice Felix 123
French National Assembly 130, 131, 135
French Revolution 128, 129, 131, 132, 138, 139, 145
General Assembly 23, 40, 44, 46, 48, 50, 51, 53, 55, 106
General Court 36, 44
Gentlemen, John Potts 49
George III 38, 87
Germany 141
Gerry, Elbridge 75, 118
Gilpin, George 49, 57
Goldberg, Justice Arthur 110
Graglia, Lino 97, 99, 102, 110
Grayson, William 32, 47, 53, 32, 47, 119, 151
Great Compromise 92, 95, 109, 119
Greece 98, 101, 141, 145
Griffin, Samuel 80, 138
Griswold v. Connecticut 110
guillotine 131
Gunnell, Thomas 49
Gunston Hall 15, 21, 29-31, 32, 47, 49, 51-53, 61, 62
             80, 82, 83, 97, 98, 117, 121, 129, 134, 138, 139, 150, 152
Hamilton, Alexander 78, 94, 100, 104, 106, 110, 132, 148, 151
Harlan, Justice John M. 125
Harrison, Gov. Benjamin 44
Henderson, Alexander 57
Henderson, Archibald 61
Henry, Patrick 32, 45, 47, 53, 59, 75, 78, 119, 149
Henry, Richard 32

INDEX

Herbert, William 49, 50
History of England 133
History of the World 133
Homer 133
Hooe and Harrison and Company 44
Hooe, Robert T. 46, 52
Horace 133
Horatio 55
House of Burgesses 18-20, 22, 23, 34, 38, 56, 82
House of Representatives, U. S. 67-70, 77, 80, 91, 158, 159
Hutcheson, Francis 135
impeachment 66, 75
India 144
Indians 20, 39
Iredell, James 78
Italian unification 141
Jamestown 17
Japan 144
Jefferson, Thomas 27, 28, 32, 46, 53, 55, 55-58, 59, 75, 78-80
      82, 93, 101, 104, 121, 123, 128-130, 132, 133, 135
           138, 144, 147, 148, 151
judicial review 84-86, 89-91, 94, 96, 97, 99-101, 105, 106, 110, 112, 113
July 14, 1789 135
justices of the peace 41, 56, 57
Juvenal 133
Lafayette 129-131, 135
Latin America 142, 144
League of Nations 142
Lee family 19
Lee, Richard Henry 32, 47, 75
Liberia 142
liberty 25, 26, 27, 29, 50, 65, 66, 73, 88, 95, 99, 105
    107-109, 111, 124, 125, 131, 132, 134-139, 141, 143, 147
        155-157, 160, 161, 163, 164, 167
Locke, John 87, 133, 135
Loudoun County 37
Lyles, William 49, 50
Madison, James 15, 27-30, 32, 40, 46, 53, 56-58
      62, 63, 67, 72-74, 75, 76, 78-80, 82, 83, 89
      94, 101-106, 109-112, 117, 121, 123, 147-149, 151
Magna Carta 124, 133
majority rule 82-87, 91, 92, 96-100
Marcus Aurelius 133
Marquis de Condorcet 129
Marshall, Chief Justice John 28, 100, 107, 120, 148, 149
Maryland 21, 23, 27, 29, 55, 61, 83, 98
Maryland Gazette 27
Mason, George (1690-1735) 20
Mason, George (1690-1735) 20, 21, 22, 82

Mason, George (1725-1792) 15-31, 32-58, 61-74, 75-127, 128-152
Mason, George 32, 33, 42, 44, 45, 47, 49, 51, 52, 54, 55, 57
    advocates Bill of Rights 15-16, 24, 28, 41, 46, 72-73
        78-81, 88, 89, 94, 97, 118-120, 124-127, 148-152, 158-160
    birth 20, 82, 128, 147
    death 151, 152
    early life 15-31
    education 22, 54, 82
    family 16, 20, 22, 29, 30, 82, 118, 150
    influence on U. S. Declaration of
        Independence 27, 132, 133-134
    influence on French Declaration of Rights of
        Man and the Citizen 128-140
    letter of resignation 51
    life 16-31, 32-58, 82, 117, 118, 128
        129, 147, 148, 150, 151
    marriage 21, 23
    Objections to the Constitution of Government 15, 23, 46, 57, 74
        75, 77-80, 89, 92, 104, 111, 149, 152, 158-160
    opposes ratification of U. S. Constitution   16, 46, 61-73, 78-81, 84
        88, 89, 120-121, 152
    political career ... 21-29, 35, 36, 45-47, 74, 75, 117, 118, 151-152
    role in U. S. Constitutional Convention ... 16, 24, 45-47, 61-73
        88, 120-121, 126-127, 148-140
    service on the Fairfax Court 32-55
    views affecting other nations 128-145
    views used in U. S. Supreme Court decisions 117-127
Mason's Neck 20
Mason Papers 55, 56-58, 73, 74
Massachusetts 79, 80, 104
Massey family 20
McCarty, Daniel 35, 39, 40, 42, 44, 47, 56
McClurg, James 62, 117
McDonald, Forrest 62, 73
Meese, Attorney General Edwin (III) 93, 99, 100, 103, 107, 110
Mercer, John 22, 56, 82, 105, 133
merchants 28, 29, 38, 44, 46, 56, 159
Militia, State .. 26,31, 33, 34, 37, 40, 56, 64, 65, 79, 87, 102, 157, 161
Miller, Helen Hill 28, 30, 31, 55
Milton, John 133
minority rights 82-85, 91, 98, 99
minority, oppression of 71, 82-113
monarchy 66, 73, 78, 118, 160
Monmouth, Battle of 130
Monroe, James 15, 28, 59, 119, 142, 151
Montaigne's *Essays* 133
Montesquieu 62
Moore, Jesse 52
Morris, Gouverneur 105, 129

Morris, Richard	130, 145
Mounier	130
Mount Vernon	17, 38, 46, 61, 117, 129
Napoleon	131
National Assembly	130, 131, 135, 136, 138
National Council	63
National League of Cities v. Usery	100
natural law	86-89, 91, 93, 97, 102, 111
natural rights	86-89, 96, 97, 99, 108, 110, 111, 163
Navigation Acts (Laws)	118, 120
New Hampshire	104, 149
New Jersey	78, 99, 122, 124
New York	29, 30, 55, 59, 98, 104, 122, 123, 145, 149
Newfoundland	142
Nigeria	145, 146
Ninth Amendment	96, 110, 111, 162
North America	38
North Carolina	29, 30, 55, 73, 78, 104, 124, 145
Occoquan Creek	82
Occoquan Plantation	21
Ohio Company	22, 38, 39, 55, 82
original intention	93, 94, 96, 99, 103, 107
Ovid	133
Paine, Thomas	128, 129, 132
Palmer, R. R.	56, 57, 129, 137, 145
parliamentary supremacy	87, 97
Payne, Edward	57
Payne, William	49, 50, 57
Pennsylvania	27, 62
Pennsylvania Evening Post	27
Pennsylvania Ledger	27
Petition of Right	133, 134
Philadelphia	16, 24, 45-47, 55, 61-64, 76, 78, 83, 85, 88, 93, 102, 105, 106, 112, 117, 119, 140, 147
Philadelphia Convention	61, 93, 105, 117
planter society	19
Plato	133
Plutarch	133
Pohick Creek	82
Pope, Alexander	133
popular election	54, 66, 67, 69, 76, 91, 92, 95, 109
Portugal	17
Potomac River	23, 61, 82, 83
Powell, Justice Lewis	122
prerogative of the royal government	41
press, freedom of	26, 29, 30, 64, 73, 74, 77, 80, 81, 103, 137, 143, 145, 150, 157, 160, 161
private property	95, 99, 137, 162
Privy Council	41

Proclamation of 1763 38
Proclamation of Neutrality 139
property 16, 20, 21, 25-27, 39, 41, 42, 50
           61, 69-71, 84, 88, 92, 95, 98, 99, 107, 108, 111, 112, 124, 131
              132, 135-138, 141, 143, 144, 155-157, 161-163, 165, 167, 170
property qualifications 92
Publius 78
Raleigh, Sir Walter 133
Randolph, Gov. Edmund 56, 57, 62, 69, 72, 73, 76, 117-119
Randolph, Gov. Beverley 53, 118, 119, 151
Randolph family 19
Reagan administration 83
Rehnquist, Chief Justice William 99
Reign of Terror 139
religion 26, 83, 95, 108, 121-123, 137, 143, 150
                                      157, 161, 167, 169, 170
representative democracy 86
republican government 71, 104, 105
right of association 65, 100, 103, 161, 136, 137, 143, 170
right to a speedy trial 124, 137
right to bear arms 150, 161
right to vote 70-71, 137, 170
Robespierre 131
Roe v. Wade 112
Roman Virtues 54
Roosevelt, Eleanor 143, 144
Roosevelt, President Franklin D. 98, 143
Rosenthal, Lewis 129
Rowland, Kate Mason 32, 39
royal governor 18
Russell, Anthony 37, 56
Russia 141
Rutland, Robert A. 24, 27, 32, 33, 51, 54
Rutledge, Justice Wiley B. 122
Salmon's *History* 133
self-incrimination 124, 150, 161
Senate 40, 47, 53, 69, 77, 80, 83, 91, 92, 109
                                 112, 119, 142, 151, 158, 159
separation of powers 69, 99, 112, 137, 165
Seventeenth Amendment 109, 162
Shakespeare 133
Sherman, Roger 75, 76, 147
shipowners 44
slave trade 76, 120, 140, 143, 149, 168
slavery ... 18, 28, 30, 31, 70, 71, 89, 108, 120, 126, 139-141, 143, 167
slaves 18, 21, 22, 25, 30, 68, 70, 82, 118, 126, 140, 141, 149, 160
slaves, importation of 70, 126
Solem v. Helm 125
South Africa 144

Spain 17, 18, 142, 145
Spanish Crown 17
Spanish Empire 17
speedy trial 26, 108, 124, 156
Stafford County 20, 23, 47
Stamp Act of 1765 .... 23, 39, 40, 83
Storing, Herbert 93, 102-104
Stuart, David 49, 57
Sugar Act of 1764 39
sumptuary laws 65
Tasso, Torquato 133
Thornburg v. Gingles 105
tobacco, taxation of 37, 38, 42, 43, 44, 48, 49
treason 67, 77, 159
trial by jury 77, 108, 150, 157, 160, 162
Truman, Harry 142
Truro Vestry 33, 39
Turkey 141
Tyler, Lyon G. 134
United Nations Universal Declaration of
  Human Rights 142-145, 165-173
Venezuela 145, 146
Virgil 133
Virginia 15-20, 22-31, 32, 38-41, 44, 46, 47, 50, 51, 53-57
          61-63, 67-70, 72, 75, 78-84, 87-90, 98, 99, 102, 104
          106, 108, 111, 117-122, 124-126, 128-135, 137, 138, 141-145
                                    149-152, 155, 157, 174
Virginia Colony 17, 18
Virginia Constitution 16, 67, 40, 53, 57
Virginia Convention 23-26, 40, 51, 81, 119, 120, 149, 150
Virginia Gazette 26
Virginia House of Delegates 23, 83
Virginia House of Delegates 83
Virginia Journal and Alexandria Advertiser 46
Virginia Legislature 106, 117
Virginia-Maryland Commission 23
Washington, George 15, 16, 27-30, 32, 38, 40, 45, 46, 51, 55
          56, 57, 62, 72, 75, 78, 82, 117, 135, 140, 145, 147, 148, 151
Washington, Bushrod 52
Weems v. United States 107
West, John 35, 39, 56
West, Roger 49, 50
Whig Principles 41, 49
William and Mary 59, 134
Willson, Beckles 129
Wilson, Woodrow 142
Wren, James 49, 57
writ of certiorari 44
Wythe, George 62, 117